Horsemanship Through Life

Other Titles by Mark Rashid

Considering the Horse:
Tales of Problems Solved and Lessons Learned

A Good Horse Is Never a Bad Color

Horses Never Lie: The Heart of Passive Leadership

Life Lessons from a Ranch Horse

Horsemanship Through Life

Mark Rashid

Foreword by *Shihan Eric Adams*

Spring Creek Press
ESTES PARK

Johnson Books
BOULDER

Published by Johnson Books, a subsidiary of Big Earth Publishing, 3005 Center Green Drive, Suite 220, Boulder, Colorado 80301. Visit our website at www.JohnsonBooks.com E-mail: books@bigearthpublishing.com

Cover and text design by Erika Echols
Cover painting by Greg Miles

9 8 7 6 5 4 3 2 1

Library of Congress Cataloging-in-Publication Data

Rashid, Mark
 Horsemanship through life / Mark Rashid.
       p. cm.
 ISBN 1-55566-364-8
 1. Horses—Colorado—Anecdotes. 2. Horsemanship—Colorado—Anecdotes. 3. Rashid, Mark. 4. Horse trainers—Colorado—Anecdotes. I. Title

SF301.R37 2005
798.2'09788—dc22
                                                                 2005024501
Printed in the United States of America

Contents

For my friend, Stacy Mendel

Foreword

It is both an honor and a pleasure to be asked by Mark to write the foreword for this groundbreaking book. I believe that when you read this book, you will find it is more than a book about horses and their riders, much more in fact. It is about one person's journey in following his passion, becoming full and then empty again, coming full circle from beginner to master, and then back to beginner again.

It is not a journey for everyone, because it is far from easy. It takes time and hard work and means sometimes having your very breath taken away from you. It is neither for the weak of heart or spirit nor for those with a closed mind. Instead it takes a willingness to learn, be humble, and acknowledge, at times, just how much you don't know.

There is an old saying in the martial arts, "When the student is ready, the teacher will appear." This is just what happened to me over twenty years ago and what has happened with so many teachers and students for hundreds of years. Sometimes it takes a while for people to work through all of the things bothering them and holding them back from what they desire to accomplish. Once they are able to come to a single, focused point, usually accepting and realizing that things are just as they are, then they can begin to deal with them in the present moment. It is this ability to deal with things in the present moment that ultimately helps us all move forward.

On the other hand, if we focus on everything that is wrong, we are not able to see what is right. If a person focuses, for instance, on all the injuries they have that won't allow them do something, they often not only make those injuries worse but hold themselves back from what they can do, which is usually considerably more than they think possible.

When Mark talked with me about his thoughts and ideas around aikido and horsemanship, the idea grabbed me right away. The work that Mark is doing is very valuable, both for the horse and rider. I have learned from my teacher that in order to truly become a martial artist, you must live your art every day of your life. Mark is doing this, both in his work and in his life. Few things are more gratifying to a teacher than to see the student take the lesson, apply it, and live it; thereby "The Way" continues.

It is the spirit the person puts into his work that is very important, more important, in fact, than the technique. We must learn from the journey, not the destination. Mark exemplifies this idea, and I am both proud and respectful of what he is accomplishing. I am also humbled to have had some small part in this journey.

I sincerely hope you are able to take in the lessons shared in this book and that your life may be improved as Mark shares his journey with you.

Osu,
Shihan Eric Adams

Eric Adams was born in Loveland, Colorado and grew up in Alaska, where he lived for twenty years before moving back to Estes Park, Colorado. Horses have been a part of Eric's life; his mother and father ran riding stables in both Glen Haven and Moraine Park, located in Rocky Mountain National Park. While in Alaska, Eric began studying the martial arts with So-Shihan Charles Scott in Fairbanks. Eventually, Eric earned black-belt ranks in Shudokan Karate, Yoshinkan Aikido, Ju-Jitsu Kobudo (weapons), Gosuku Ryu Karate, and Hojutsu (the art of shooting). He now has a dojo in Estes Park. He also works at the MacGregor Ranch, an historic working cattle ranch and youth education center.

Introduction

I'm not exactly sure when I first used the term "horsemanship through life," but I do remember why I used it. It was in response to a question a lady asked me regarding what I thought the most important factor in becoming a good horseman was. I told her it was finding a way to practice horsemanship in your everyday life, not just when you were with your horse. The woman looked somewhat perplexed at the answer.

I went on to explain that from what I often see, many horse people (particularly the "backyard" horse person) really only practice their horsemanship when they're with their horses. They may go through the rest of their day yelling at the kids, arguing with co-workers, inadvertently butting in line at the supermarket, or having a bout of road rage on the highway. Then they just assume they can work with their horses and suddenly become patient, calm, aware, and understanding.

Or, on the other end of the spectrum, they may go through their day verbally or mentally negotiating every little thing that comes up (even when negotiation isn't appropriate or needed). Yet they think they can approach their horses and somehow become calmly assertive, if and when it's necessary.

The biggest problem is that most people who own horses these days are pretty limited in the time they are able to spend with them. It may be anywhere from a few minutes to a couple of hours per day, if that. The rest of their time is spent on the routines of their everyday lives, which seldom have anything to do with horses. While maybe an hour or so per day is spent with their horses, as much as twenty-three hours are spent away from them. Yet, in my opinion, it is actually those other twenty-three hours that can be the most beneficial, as far as improving our horsemanship!

You see, when we are with our horses, we have an opportunity to spend time working with the normal tools of the horsemanship trade—halters, lead ropes, saddles, bridles, and so forth. But when we are away from our horses, we have the opportunity to hone the greatest horsemanship tools we have—our minds and bodies.

For me, being good at horsemanship isn't just about how we do things when we are with our horses. It is also about how we do things when we are away from them. Even someone who is only able to spend fifteen minutes a day with his horse can be working on horsemanship throughout the rest of the day. After all, the qualities required to be good with horses are the same qualities required to be good at life in general, and vice versa.

Chances are real good that if a person is indecisive, angry, scattered, hesitant, belligerent, argumentative, bossy, or impatient in everyday life, he is bound to bring those same qualities to his horsemanship, and in turn, his horse will tend to reflect those qualities. By the same token, if a person is patient, calm, willing, quiet, self-confident, focused, and dependable, it is more than likely to be those qualities the horse will reflect.

Whether positive or negative, it is almost always those qualities we practice in our everyday lives that have the most powerful effect on our horsemanship. Of course, the greatest thing about all this is that not only do we have the power to choose the qualities we want to exhibit in our everyday lives, we also have the power—and the time—to practice them!

For me, the idea of "horsemanship through life" took on a whole new meaning several years ago, when I found myself bothered by some old physical injuries, as well as some seemingly unrelated personal issues I was going through. Without realizing it, I began to allow these issues to creep into pretty much every aspect of my life, including my horsemanship, and the results ended up being, shall we say, less than favorable.

For a time, I tried to fix the problems in my horsemanship without addressing the other issues, only to find that not only did things not improve, to some degree they actually became worse. Only when I began looking outside the world of horsemanship and took a path that ultimately led me into martial arts, did I begin to find the answers I was looking for. Consequently everything began to fall back into place in a positive way.

Going through this experience firsthand helped me see that the concept of "horsemanship through life" could be much more than just a way of *doing* things with horses . . . it could actually become a way of *being* with horses. As such, my hope is that in some small way the account you are about to read will be helpful to you—whether you're a professional horseperson, a backyard horseperson, or just someone who admires horses from afar—and that it might also help illustrate just how much power the idea of horsemanship through life can hold for us all.

—M.R.

When we listen to our horses, we get an education.
When we don't, we get experience.

—Mark Rashid

The Sound

It was a strange sound but not totally unfamiliar. I paused to give it some thought . . . trying to place this unusual noise, which was almost ghostly in nature. It was as if somebody was saying "hi" in a very odd way—not the normal greeting you would give someone on the street, but rather a long, drawn-out "hiiiiiiiiieeee" in a breathless, almost hoarse voice. The "hi" slowly faded out, and then I could hear another one. There had been several already, although I couldn't tell exactly how many, and each one seemed louder than the last.

I tried to remember the last time I heard this unusual resonance, and at first, I drew a complete blank. Finally, after what seemed like an awfully long time, the image of where I had last heard it came rushing into my mind, as if a bucket of cold water had been dumped on my head.

It was sort of a ritual. Two or three times a month, the old man I worked for when I was a kid, Walter Pruitt, would go to this horse sale or that one and buy a few horses. The horses he brought back were usually not what you'd call the cream of the crop. In fact, they were almost always horses with some pretty substantial training issues, including some confirmed "buckers." Because of the nature of their training "issues," the old man was almost always able to buy the horses for dirt cheap . . . and sometimes even less.

Once he had the horses back at the barn, he'd have me get on each one and go for a ride. He seldom told me what was wrong with the horses, but since I was only twelve years old, he probably didn't see the need. It didn't really matter anyway, because in many cases it would turn out there was actually very little wrong with them. Even though the previous owners had deemed them "problem" horses, many of them would be just as nice as you please. If we didn't really find anything wrong with a horse, we would work with it for a while and get it going pretty good. Then he would turn around and sell it for a substantial profit.

However, not all of the horses were that quiet when I got on them. Every once in a while we'd come across one that, for whatever reason, wasn't real interested in carrying someone around on its back. Many of these horses would go to jumping or bucking right off the bat for no apparent reason, some as soon as I'd put my foot in the stirrup. Others would wait until I was settled in the saddle before they blew; still others worked just fine for several minutes before uncorking.

Oddly enough, one of the things the old man was interested in seeing when I climbed on one of those horses was how well the horse bucked, if it did. You see, the horses that bucked "good" were destined for a career in the rodeo after he sold them to a stock contractor buddy of his. It was a way for the old man to save those horses from a sure trip to the killers. They might not have been able to become a good riding horse, but at least they could go out and do what they did best . . . and that was buck.

The old man used to say this about the lives of rodeo bucking horses: "Not a bad job. Work eight seconds a week; then sit in a pasture and eat green grass the rest of the time. I hope I can find a job like that someday."

At any rate, I'd been on quite a few of these sale horses over a two-month period, and most of the rides had been pretty uneventful, with one or two of the horses hopping around a little bit, but nothing major. But on an unusually cold and windy summer day, he had me climb on a big, gray, four-year-old gelding. The horse stood about sixteen hands tall and weighed around 1,300 pounds. He was certainly quiet enough on the ground. He let me catch him without any problem, brushing and saddling weren't an issue, and even getting on his back seemed okay to him. The problem came when I asked him to move . . . and what a problem it was.

I gave the big horse a soft squeeze with my heels, but he didn't budge. I squeezed a little harder, but still no response. I bumped him with my heels and felt his body tighten, but he still didn't move. I bumped him harder, and that's when it happened. It started small enough with the horse grunting a little and taking one very stiff step forward. He paused for a brief second, then gathered himself up in what seemed to be a very unnatural, ball-like position, squealed loudly, and launched himself high into the air.

The jump initially drove me deep into the saddle. The G-forces kept me there until we reached our maximum height, and then we began our descent. To say I was surprised by the horse's actions would be a huge understatement, and I had instinctively grabbed for the saddle horn while we were on our way up. On the way down, however, I felt myself lose my seat, and I tried to use my grip on the saddle horn to recapture it. We landed hard, pitching me forward onto the horse's neck, and no sooner had we lit than he reared up and jumped back into the air. My upper body was immediately forced backward when he jumped, which almost righted me in the saddle, but then the big gray added a little twist to his body while he was in the air. That was just a bit too much for me to handle.

We parted ways in mid-air, the gelding going off to the right, me going off to the left. Much to my surprise, I landed relatively harmlessly on the top rail of the fence. When I lit, my arms and head went over the rail, while my body stayed inside the fence. My armpits ended up supporting the majority of my weight, while my left foot caught a rail near the ground. I did hit pretty hard, bruising the inside of my arms, my upper chest, my chin, and my left thigh, but other than that, I was relatively unscathed and just happy to be able to walk away from a wreck that could have been a whole lot worse. The old man, however, was apparently not impressed.

On more than one occasion, the old man had voiced his displeasure at the fact that when I got in trouble riding I would sometimes "grab leather." In particular, I grabbed the saddle horn. This time was no exception. I was still hanging on the fence, and the horse was still charging around the pen, alternating squeals and bucks with airs above the ground, when the old man came up to me.

"Grabbin' leather ain't no way to learn how to sit a horse," he said, with a hint of disgust in his voice. "If a man rides so bad a horse gets him off when he jumps, then that man deserves to be on the ground, fair and square."

Easy for you to say, I thought, as I hung there on the fence by my armpits. *You weren't the one getting pitched around like a rag doll.*

"You learn how to ride better," he said, as he walked away, "and you won't have to worry about getting thrown."

I had watched the old man ride many times, and the thing that always struck me about the way he rode was the ease with which a horse could move beneath him. He made riding look effortless, as if the horse and he were one. Shortly after coming off the big gray gelding, I remember sitting on the fence, watching the old man ride a young horse for about an hour-and-a-half. There wasn't anything special about what he was doing with the horse, and the horse was sure quiet enough. So it was somewhat of a surprise when I realized about halfway through the ride that I'd been smiling pretty much the whole time I'd been watching him.

At the time I didn't know why I was smiling, and it took me a number of years to figure it out. I finally realized the reason I couldn't keep from smiling was simply because they looked so good together. No stress, no stiffness, no anxiety, no tension, and no force. Just a man and a horse moving effortlessly together, the way it should be.

About then, I started to understand what the old man had been trying to say to me about my riding. For quite a while all I *thought* he was saying was, "don't grab leather." I didn't really know why he didn't want me to grab leather, other than perhaps that wasn't the way real horsemen rode. I thought I *needed* to grab leather in order to stay on the horse when things went south.

And therein lies the problem with my whole thought process. I was trying to stay *on* the horse, not *with* the horse. When the old man rode, he rode *with* the horse. When I rode, I rode *on* the horse, which very often turned into riding against the horse. When you ride against the horse, it often makes it almost impossible to move in the saddle. Once you stop moving while riding, you become very stiff and rigid—sometimes almost mannequin-like. Imagine for a moment what a mannequin would look like if it were sitting on top of a trotting horse or, for that matter, how a horse would feel trying to trot with a mannequin on its back!

Well, it turns out that was how I was riding—stiff and unmoving in the saddle. Of course, the stiffer you are in the saddle, the easier it is to become part of an unscheduled dismount. You see, what I didn't realize was that if I grabbed the saddle horn to stay on, I was pretty much already off anyway. Even though I may not have been off to the point where I was on the ground, I was still working against the horse instead of with him. By grabbing the horn I would end up with a huge stiffness or brace that started in the hand clutched on the horn and transferred all the way through the rest of my body, producing the mannequin effect. Once that happened, it was just a matter of time before I'd hit the ground. Which, truth be known, I was actually doing with some frequency.

Well, once I figured all that out, I decided it was time to try to change the way I rode. I spent more time watching the old man ride, trying to see what exactly it was he was doing in the saddle that allowed him to stay with any horse he rode. The more I watched, the more it dawned on me it wasn't what he was doing in the saddle that made his riding appear so effortless, it was what he wasn't doing.

He wasn't pushing his feet hard into the stirrups for balance, like I had been doing since I started riding the bucking horses. Rather, his legs just sort of hung loose around the horse's sides with his feet relaxed in the stirrups. No matter what the horse did, whether walking quietly down a trail or pitching a huge fit of some kind, his legs always seemed very loose. Because his legs were loose, the rest of his body stayed loose, and because his body stayed loose, he was able to move with the horse.

Armed with this new information, I started trying to mimic the old man's way of riding. From that point forward, as soon as I'd get in the saddle, I'd take a minute and relax my legs before asking the horse to move. The hard part was trying to keep them loose during the ride. It wasn't all that long, however, before relaxing my legs all the time became easier and easier for me. Not surprisingly, that way of riding began to feel much better, and looking back, it was actually the way I'd ridden when I first began just a few years earlier. It was only after getting on a couple of horses that went to bucking unexpectedly that I had begun riding with my legs (and therefore the rest of my body) braced. After a while that way of riding had turned into a habit.

Interestingly, once I started riding with my legs more relaxed, I slowly began noticing stiffness in other parts of my body, in particular my shoulders, arms, and hands. I figured I'd better get rid of that stiffness, too, and as a result, it wasn't long before I was working on relaxing my entire body while in the saddle. Once I was able to do that consistently, I noticed my balance in the saddle improving and then my overall riding ability improving. Things were definitely on the upturn!

Over time, my confidence in my riding ability began to grow substantially. This was due mostly to the fact that I hadn't grabbed leather in months and still hadn't come off a horse, even when the horse had gotten a little "froggy." In fact, since coming off that big gray, I'd been on a couple of horses that jumped just as big, if not bigger, and had no trouble at all staying with them. But I think there was also another reason I was feeling so good. Only recently the old man had given me a rare compliment on my seat, saying he had been impressed with the way I had been riding lately. I was on cloud nine for days afterwards.

A few months after that, however, things went a little sideways. It was late spring and most of the snow had melted. What was left was thawing pretty quickly, and muddy water ran in torrents all over the ranch. The one good thing about that time of the year was that the pastures were starting to turn from the dull brown of winter to a light shade of green. When the wind blew just right, you could even smell new grass pushing its way through the spring mud.

Late that morning after my chores were done, the old man asked me to ride a little bay mare named Sissie out on the trail. She was a horse I'd ridden many times before, and we had always gotten along nicely. She was one of the project horses the old man had picked up the summer before, and she hadn't been much of a problem from the first day I rode her. In fact, the old man had decided that he was going to put her up for sale. The only problem was that the majority of the work we'd done with her had been in the arena. We'd had a particularly snowy winter and getting her on the trails had been next to impossible.

While she had never really been difficult to ride or handle, on this particular day she seemed a bit out of sorts almost from the minute I went out to catch her. I had no sooner put the halter on to lead her to the barn than she was laying her ears back and swishing her tail. When I saddled her, she stomped her feet and gave me nasty looks. When I went to get on, she moved away from me a number of times. Her behavior worried me a little, as it was pretty much out of the ordinary, and when I mentioned it to the old man, he seemed a little concerned as well.

"Don't do very much with her, then," he told me. "Just take her down to the second gate and back. See how she feels after that. If she still isn't right, put her up, and we'll look at her again tomorrow." I nodded and began to ride away.

"Nothing more than a walk," he said, almost as an afterthought.

The second gate wasn't all that far away, maybe a half mile, and it was flat ground all the way there and back. We hadn't gone very far when I noticed the little mare wasn't moving right. Something in her hindquarters seemed to have a little glitch—not quite a limp, but not a full stride either. I thought about taking her back, but because it didn't seem all that bad, I decided to keep going, even though her ears had been perpetually pinned in dissatisfaction.

I guess we were about three-quarters of the way to the second gate when Sissie suddenly planted her feet, refusing to take another step. I urged her forward, but she wouldn't move. Knowing something wasn't right, I decided just to get off and lead her back, rather than trying to fight with her about going forward when she wasn't feeling good. We were in a particularly bad area anyway, with most of the ground covered with stumps and fallen timber from the previous autumn when a microburst had come through one afternoon and knocked down about a half-acre's worth of the trees along the trail.

When I took my right foot out of the stirrup and began getting off, the little mare suddenly exploded. Needless to say, I was immediately in a very precarious situation. I was half off, half on, with both hands on the saddle horn and my right leg sort of hooked around the cantle of the saddle. She jumped hard sideways, away from me, and then threw in two very big bucks. I was off before I knew it, sailing extremely high over her head and doing what felt like a half-somersault.

On my way down I remember thinking, *Boy, this is gonna hurt.* And I was right. I landed on my back with a hard jolt, a jolt so hard it was like nothing else I'd ever felt in my life. Luckily, I missed all the fallen trees that were scattered around, but I did hit the ground at probably the only spot within a five-mile radius that hadn't gone through the spring thaw yet. That one spot, shaded by the only two trees still left standing after the microburst went through, was rock-hard and unforgiving.

The air was knocked out of my lungs with tremendous force, and I lay there dazed and unable to breathe. It seemed like minutes before I was able to move, and when I did, it was to roll over on my right side, toward the trail. My vision was blurred and I tried to draw a breath, but no air would go in. I could hear the little mare's hoof beats—she was leaving in a hurry, heading back toward the barn, I guessed.

My upper back started to ache . . . bad. I closed my eyes and tried to pull in another breath, but still nothing would go in. I could feel a low-level panic begin to set in. A frenzied whinny from the mare faded in the distance. I opened my eyes and could see more clearly, but nothing I was seeing made sense. I could see trees in the distance, but I wasn't sure what they were called. There were also a lot of trees lying on the ground. That was strange because they looked a lot like the ones that were standing. I couldn't figure out why some of them were standing upright and some weren't. Everything was a little foggy.

I tried again to take in a breath, and this time some air painfully went into my lungs. But just as quickly as that air went in, my body forced it right back out. I would find out later that that particular involuntary reaction was my body trying to make some attempt at breathing normally after being unnaturally deprived of air.

I took in another breath, and again it was forced right back out. I struggled to roll over and slowly pushed myself onto my hands and knees. I sucked in another breath and out it came. I tried to cough, but that simply wasn't going to work at all. I tried to focus on a small spot on the ground and then suck in some more air. It went in and then came back out, this time a little slower but still very labored. It was about then, I believe, when I became vaguely aware for the first time that I was hearing some strange noise.

That was the very first time I heard that unusual sound—that somewhat ghostly noise, as if somebody was trying to say "hi," a long and drawn out "hiiiiiiiiieeee," in that breathless, almost hoarse voice.

And here I was, some thirty-four years later, hearing the sound again. The circumstances were eerily similar. I was on my hands and knees in the dirt, staring down at a small spot on the ground and trying to take in air. At first, I was a little hazy as to how I ended up in the dirt or even where I was, for that matter.

I looked off to my right and saw a slightly crumpled, light-gray Resistol lying upsidedown in the dirt not far away.

That's my hat, something in the dark recesses of my brain told me.

Instinctively, I tried to crawl over to where the hat rested. However, I no sooner tried to move my hand toward the hat than a massive pain shot through my left side. The pain instantly stopped me, and in reflex my right hand quickly went to that area. Then there was that strange sound again.

This time, with the cobwebs beginning to clear, I came to realize the sound I was hearing was loud—extremely, almost unnaturally loud. In fact, it seemed electronically-enhanced-loud, as if it were being broadcast through a P.A. system. Through the mental fog, I began to see the entire situation, as it slowly pieced itself together.

The first thing I figured out was that the unusual noise I was hearing was the sound of me trying to catch my breath. The reason I was having so much trouble breathing was that I had just come off a horse in what must have been a pretty spectacular wreck. I was having trouble regaining my senses because, when I landed, I must have had my bell rung a little. I couldn't breathe because I'd gotten the wind knocked out of me.

Then the last piece of the puzzle hazily slipped into place. The reason that noise was so unusually loud was because it was being broadcast throughout the indoor arena I was in, via the wireless microphone I was wearing.

Aw, man, I thought to myself, *I'm wearing a mic.*

I looked down at the pocket of the wool vest I was wearing, and sure enough, there was a transmitter for a wireless microphone in the pocket. I reached up and found the small mouthpiece of the headset near my mouth.

That means I'm teaching a clinic. I slowly shook my head in disgust. *I just came off a horse while I was teaching a clinic!*

I reached down and fumbled for the on/off switch on the transmitter. It took a couple seconds, but I finally found it and flicked it off. Immediately the inside of the arena became quiet, almost too quiet. I could still hear the sound of me trying to catch my breath, but other than that, there was very little sound at all. I began to look around in an attempt to regain my bearings. There was a woman coming toward me with a very concerned look on her face. Someone else was walking next to her.

"Stay down for a moment," I heard a voice with an English accent say.

"Are you all right?" There was another voice with an accent.

I forced myself over and grabbed my hat. I shook off the dirt and smoothed the wrinkles out a little before putting it back on my head.

"I'm okay," I grunted. "Just got the wind knocked out of me. How's the horse?"

"Are you sure you're all right?"

"Yeah, I'm fine," was my airless reply.

I may have been getting my senses back, but for the life of me, I couldn't figure out why everyone was speaking with an English accent. Then, as I slowly scanned the entire arena, I could see the big horse I must have been riding standing off to the side, and the somewhat shell-shocked auditors behind a small, makeshift fence at the other end of the arena. Folks were dressed a little differently than what I was used to seeing. The inside of the arena looked different, too. The people who were talking were speaking with an English accent. Then it finally dawned on me . . . I was in England! For crying out loud, I just fell off a horse while I was teaching a clinic in England!

My very first thought was, *How did that happen? How the heck did I come off? I haven't come off a horse in years!*

Well, as it turns out, while I had not actually come off a horse in quite a while, the truth of the matter was, I had been working up to a lot worse for a lot longer. This fall was just a wake-up call—one I quickly found I'd better pay attention to.

2

Top of the Spiral

That arena in England was both literally and figuratively a long way from the old man's little horse ranch where I spent so much time when I was a kid. When I stop to think about it, it actually boggles my mind. As I grew up, working with horses was just something that I enjoyed doing, like playing basketball with my friends or hanging out in the schoolyard or eating supper. I never saw it as anything special. I certainly never thought it would ever come to anything.

In fact, there was a time in my life when I stepped away from horses for a while and played music professionally. When I did get back into horses after that self-imposed layoff, it was in a rather inauspicious way, working with one horse here, another there, taking trail rides while on vacation, and so on. Eventually I went back to working at various ranches and dude operations and ultimately moved from guiding rides and tending cattle to managing the horse herds and even becoming livery manager and ranch foreman. In each case, when it came to my work with the horses, I always stayed with three main principles, which I had subconsciously picked up all those years ago while working for the old man.

The first was to always try to work with the horse, not against him, whether I was on the horse's back or working with him on the ground. The other two were very simple principles that took me years to understand. I suppose one of the reasons it took me so long to grasp them was the way they were originally presented to me.

13

❊

It had been raining hard for two days straight, and by the time the deluge finally came to an end, the ground was pretty much saturated and the horses' pasture was turning into a soupy mess. The old man decided to take the herd of about forty head off the pasture and separate them into three large, dry-lot pens until the ground in the pasture dried out a bit. That way the new spring grass would stand a chance to come up healthy.

These particular three pens were on a bit of a slope, so the rainwater had drained off pretty quickly. They were still a little greasy and we were going to have to throw hay for a couple days, but at least we didn't have to worry about ruining our summer feed.

The old man brought the herd in with a great little horse named Blue. Blue was short and very stocky, an old bulldogging-style horse—low to the ground, tons of power, and quick on his feet. The plan was to gather the herd, take them through the south pasture gate, through the middle pasture, turn them east toward the barn, and move them into the first, relatively large round pen by the barn. There we'd separate them into the three dry lots. I was on foot, and my job was to close the gates behind the old man and the horses after they went through.

Everything went off pretty much without a hitch. The old man had eased the horses out of the south pasture without ever breaking them out of a walk. He masterfully turned them east and drove them to the pen by the barn. The gate to the pen was already open, and he moved them in with very little effort. Then came the hard part.

The old man wanted to sort the herd, putting the youngsters in one pen and two different groups of friends in the other pens. That way, there hopefully wouldn't be too much trouble between the horses at feeding time, seeing as how we were going to be throwing hay for a few days. Within a matter of minutes, he had the eight youngsters cut out of the herd and standing on the west side of the pen, near the three gates to the dry lots. He had me open the middle gate, and with a couple of subtle moves by him and his horse, the youngsters walked right in. I closed the gate behind them.

He began to separate the remainder of the herd into two groups, trying to keep the horses that liked each other together. He quickly had one group standing quietly on the right side of the pen and the other group on the left side. He had me open the gate on the left, so he could move that group through.

The problem with that particular gate was that it wouldn't swing open or closed very well. The fit had always been a little loose anyway, and now with all the rain, the wood had swelled so much the end of the gate sagged right down into the mud. It was a heavy wooden gate on top of that, and in order for me to get it open, I had to lift the end with both hands and sort of half drag and half hop it open enough for the horses to get through.

It took me quite a while to get the gate open wide enough, and when I finally did, the old man moved the horses toward it. However, as soon as he began moving that little bunch, the other group began to follow.

"Stay right there near the gate," he told me. "If that other group tries to follow this one into that pen, just step in front of them and get them turned back toward me."

"Step in front of them?" I questioned with a little concern. "What if they go to run me over?"

"Aw, don't worry," he said confidently. "They won't run you over."

"Okay," I replied, in a far less confident tone.

I suppose everybody has a story or two about how they arrived at a point in their lives when, out of the blue, they heard the little voice. You know, the one you hear when you're about to do something that may have sounded like a good idea at first, but upon reflection, actually seems to be a monumentally bad idea. Well, this was one of those times for me.

There I was, standing near the gate with the horses just starting to file through into the dry lot. Suddenly, the youngsters in the pen next door decided it was time to kick up their heels and take off running for the far end. The horses that had been moving nicely through the gate took one look at those colts and decided they might as well go along. Just like that, they took off running, too.

Well, those horses stampeding through the gate acted like a sort of vacuum for the horses still in the big round pen, sucking them toward the open gate and me. The horses in the round pen began to trot and then broke into a run about twenty feet from me. The old man was out of position to cut them all off, although he was able to get the bunch cut in two and turn about half of them away from the gate.

About that time, the little voice began talking to me. It said something like, *Maybe this would be a good time to get out of the way.* For a second I contemplated doing just that, grabbing the top rail of the gate and swinging up on it. But it was only for a second. The old man's instructions to "step in front of them and get them turned back" echoed in my head as I jumped out from my position next to the gate into the middle of the opening. From what I understood the old man say, that would pretty much be all I'd need to do to get a bunch of stampeding horses to stop stampeding. Obviously, my take on what he said was completely wrong, and in very short order those horses had gone right over the top of me on their way to join their buddies in the dry lot.

On their way past, they unceremoniously knocked me back into the gate, where I lost my footing and fell down. One horse just barely nicked my calf with his hoof as he tried to jump over me, while another clipped the left side of my rib cage. Neither injury was serious, barely even leaving a bruise, but that didn't help the anger that suddenly boiled up inside me as I lay there, face first in the mud. I pushed myself up onto my knees and looked down at my mud-caked clothes, shaking more mud from the palms of my hands.

"Dang it!" I exclaimed.

From behind me, I could hear the old man laughing. I turned around to see him holding the remaining horses near the other side of the pen.

"You're a sight!" he chuckled.

"Oh, yeah?" I said defiantly as I slipped to my feet. "I thought you said they wouldn't run me over!"

"There was your mistake, right there," he was still chuckling a bit. "You shoulda listened to them horses instead of me."

I had heard the old man say many times that you should always listen to what the horse is trying to say. I have to admit that at the time I didn't really understand what he meant by that. The thought that a horse would try to "talk" to a human was so foreign to me that it just didn't make much sense. As a result, I had sort of stopped trying to figure out the meaning behind it.

I think the old man knew that particular concept was something I didn't understand, too, and I can't prove it, but I think he may have set up that whole situation just to get me thinking a little harder about it. Whether that was actually the case or not, I guess I'll never know, but it certainly was the outcome. One thing is sure—from that day forward, I began looking at horses and their behavior a whole lot differently than I had before.

Something else happened that day that was also pretty important for me. You see, for a long time I just couldn't help feeling that the old man had set me up to fail, and I didn't like it. After all, I trusted him when he told me those horses wouldn't run me over. That was why I went ahead and jumped in front of them in the first place. How was I to know any different? I was not only pretty young at the time, but I also had very little experience with horses to base my decision on. As a result, I put all my trust and, ultimately, my safety, in what the old man told me.

It was easy for me to place my trust in him without thinking the situation through on my own. After all, at my age I had already been programmed, if you will, to follow instructions blindly. You see, from a very early age, kids are taught not to question people who are older. If kids are told to do something and told it will be all right if they do it, they just assume it will be. In other words, kids are taught to trust an older person's judgment, not necessarily their own.

Now, granted, while we are growing up, we all need positive guidance from adults so we don't go out and get ourselves killed. But, if we go too long without being able to make decisions on our own, we never learn how to make them at all, whether good or bad. I think the old man could see that I wasn't making decisions for myself, and when it comes to working with horses, that is not a good place to be. So, while at first I felt as though the old man had set me up to fail that day, I figured out that what he had actually done was set me up to succeed.

So there they are—the three major principles that have stayed with me all this time.

Work with the horse, not against him.

Always listen to what the horse is trying to say.

And always think for yourself.

In theory, these are very simple ideas. However, they can prove a bit more difficult to put in practice.

Some people are a little surprised to hear that I have led a very sheltered life when it comes to working with horses. As a kid I worked solely with the old man at his place. I never went to other ranches or stables, so my view on how horses should be worked was very narrow and basically came from his perspective. As I grew older and began working at other operations, much of the riding I did was on horses already trained for working cattle or guiding.

As time went on, I was often put in charge of the horses on the ranches where I worked, and I did much of the training work by myself. With nobody else around to give me input, I worked with the horses as I had back when I was a kid, which was basically the "fly by the seat of your pants" method. When I came upon a difficult problem with a horse, I would just go about my business and try to find a way around it. Seldom did I rely on any one technique in a given situation, simply because I had never really studied different techniques.

Now don't get me wrong here. Technique is definitely important when it comes to working with horses, and in order to accomplish certain work with them, you need to have a good grasp of a number of techniques. However, if you are *only* a student of technique, then the options become very limited. On the other hand, when you are a student of the horse, the options are unlimited.

As with anything, there are advantages and disadvantages to working alone, particularly when it comes to working with horses.

The biggest disadvantage is that you have no one to bounce ideas off or to check in with from time to time to see if you're on the right track. As a result, there is always an awful lot of trial and error going on, which slows the work down considerably. On the other hand, one of the biggest advantages of working alone is that there is never anyone there telling you something won't work. As a result, the sky is the limit for things you can try and, ultimately, for things you will discover.

This was certainly the case in my situation. Because I had nobody around telling me the things I was doing were wrong, I never knew they were supposed to be wrong, so I went ahead and did them anyway. Very often these things that were supposed to be wrong or ineffective actually worked just fine, given time. It was years later, once I started getting out and away from my relatively solitary work on ranches, that I began hearing how I shouldn't do this thing or that thing because it would never work, even though I had known for years that it would.

Over time, my work on ranches expanded out into the real world with real people. It happened very slowly and started by word of mouth, when somehow someone saw me work with a horse on the ranch I was at. That person went home and told one of his friends. Then that person called me up to see if I would have a look at his horse. So, I'd go have a look, work with the horse for a while, and go home. A few weeks later I'd get a call from someone else who wanted me to look at his horse. Then a few weeks later I'd get another call, and so on.

One thing led to another, and after several years, I found myself out doing clinics all over the country and eventually all over the world. That's when things began to change for me.

Like I said, pretty much all my life I was quite sheltered when it came to working with horses. As a result, I was completely ignorant of other trainers and the methods and techniques that were out there. So, when I went out to do clinics, I would do the work just as I had while I was back at the ranch. In short, I had an "anything goes" attitude. I would watch what was going on between the horse and rider and then often make up a solution as we went.

Usually these solutions were so simple the riders had overlooked them. They had been trying to "technique" their way through the problems, as opposed to thinking them through to find a way simply to listen to the horse and work with it, instead of against it.

While I was working in New Mexico, a fellow by the name of Jim brought his gelding into the round pen. He had the horse saddled and ready to ride, but he told me he wanted to do some ground work first.

"What kind of ground work do you want to do?" I asked.

"I want to work on his disrespectfulness," he replied.

The horse was standing quietly by Jim's side; his head was down and he looked like he was ready to take a nap.

Now, before I go any further, I should probably point out that the idea a horse would be "disrespectful" was one of those things I was completely ignorant of prior to performing clinics. I had never heard that term used to describe interactions between horses and people, so it came as a complete surprise to me the first time I heard it at that clinic in New Mexico.

It never occurred to me that it was possible for horse to even *want* to be disrespectful to a human. It is one of those things that didn't make sense to me then, and truth be known, it still doesn't make sense to me.

"So," I questioned almost tentatively, "you feel he's being disrespectful right now?"

Jim looked down at his napping gelding and then smiled.

"Well, no," he half chuckled. "Not this second. It's more when I ask him to do this . . . "

Jim stepped to the horse's hindquarters and pushed his fingertips into the horse's rib cage, right in front of his flank. The horse responded by pinning his ears, stomping his hind foot, swishing his tail, and moving his hindquarters away. Jim stepped toward him and, once again, pressed his fingertips into the horse's rib cage. Again the horse pinned his ears, stomped his hind foot, swished his tail, and moved his hindquarters away.

"See what I mean?" Jim asked.

"And what part of that do you feel is the disrespectful part?" I asked.

He went back to the horse's flank and pressed on him once again. The horse pinned his ears and swished his tail.

"That," he blurted. "Right there. That swishing his tail. And he's pinning his ears. Why is he doing that? He should just disengage his hindquarters and move over."

"I see. And you feel he's being disrespectful when he does the ear pinning and tail swishing, even though he's moving when you ask?"

"Don't you?"

"Well," I went on, "I don't know. How long have you been asking him to disengage his hindquarters like that?"

"You mean when did I first start teaching it?"

"Yes."

"I don't know," he said thoughtfully. "A year ago. Maybe a year-and-a-half."

"I see," I replied. "And how often do you ask him to do it?"

"I guess three or four times on each side before I go to get on him."

"Every time you get on?"

"Yes."

"And how often do you ride him? How many times a week?"

"Usually three or four times a week," he said. "Sometimes more."

"So, three or four times every week," I started, "for the last year-and-a half, you've been putting your hand on him like that and asking him to move over, and you do that three or four times on each side every time you get on him?"

"Yes, that's right," he replied.

"I see."

"So," he questioned, "how do I get him to stop being so disrespectful?"

"I guess if it were me," I told him, "I'd quit asking him to do that."

Jim stood quietly for a few seconds and then smiled and nodded.

"Okay." He looked down at his horse's head before looking back at me. "But no, really. How do I get him to stop?"

"Don't ask him to do that anymore," I repeated.

Jim looked at me like I was crazy. I could see the wheels turning. I could almost hear the question going through his mind—*I paid good money for THIS?*

"He's got it," I went on. "He knows what you want when you put your hand on him, there. You don't have to practice it anymore. It's making him mad. He doesn't see the point of doing it over and over for no reason."

"What do you mean, 'no reason'?" Jim sounded a little aggravated. "I asked him to do it. That should be reason enough."

"Well, let me put it another way," I said. "When you were in grade school, how many grades did you go through before your teachers stopped asking you what one plus one was?"

Jim stood without answering, perhaps thinking it was a rhetorical question.

"Was it third grade? Fourth grade? Seventh grade?"

"Well, no," he interrupted. "I don't think anybody asked me that past first grade."

"There you go," I nodded. "Your horse is in the same boat. Disengaging is something he learned in first grade. Now he's in high school and you keep asking him what one plus one is. It's aggravating to him."

Jim looked at his horse, then back at me.

"He knows this," I repeated. "You don't need to keep asking him to do it. It'll be there when you need it. There'll come a time when you'll ask him to move over because you actually *need* him to do it for some reason, and I expect he'll go just fine without so much as an ear flick."

Jim looked unconvinced but seemed to accept my explanation, so we moved on to other things. His horse was actually a very nice fellow, and over the next couple of days, we got quite a bit accomplished. Jim did as I asked and refrained from asking his horse to disengage. Surprisingly, he said his horse seemed happier overall and even seemed more quiet and willing while he was riding than he had before. Jim even wondered aloud to himself whether stopping the disengaging routine had had such a dramatic effect on the horse that it changed his attitude while being ridden.

On the last day of the clinic, Jim rode his horse into the arena, and he was already smiling.

"What's up?" I asked.

"You'll never believe it," he said, with a big grin on his face. "I was brushing him over by the trailer, and I accidentally dropped my brush. Without even thinking, I asked him to move his back end over so I could pick it up, and he did, just as nice as could be. No ear pinning, no foot stomping, no tail swishing, nothing. Just stepped right over, soft and quiet."

Jim would later tell me he had come to the clinic looking for some technique to fix what he believed was disrespect from his horse. He had been studying different techniques for so long, in one way or another, he just assumed another technique would be the answer. He never dreamed the answer would be to simply stop what he was doing.

This is the type of thing I feel working by myself for all those years really helped me with. That is, looking for a simple solution to issues that, at the time, may seem insurmountable. I found more times than not, it was indeed the simple solution that was the most effective.

As I started bringing this idea into the clinics, almost right away people began to see there could be a benefit in it. As folks began to have more success in the clinics, word of mouth spread, and soon I had long waiting lists for the clinics.

In turn, I was suddenly getting a lot of what I saw as undue credit for something I was sure many riders could have figured out for themselves, if they would only take the time. At first, getting this credit was a little uncomfortable for me to accept, because it just didn't seem right. But, after repeatedly hearing my clients tell me what a great experience they'd had at the clinics, I guess I started to get used to it, and as time passed, I actually started to believe I deserved the credit.

Looking back, it was getting all that positive feedback from riders over an extended period of time that started me on a slow downward spiral, culminating with my being face down in the dirt in an indoor arena in England. While I believe that the positive feedback was the beginning of my fall, there were certainly other factors that came into play as well. Recognizing these factors and then trying to sort them out . . . well, that was another matter.

But sort them out, I would. And once I did, it not only took me past the downward spiral, but also opened doors I never even knew existed. Before that could happen, though, a number of other things first had to fall into place.

3

Slippery Slope

Pretty much anyone who has been around horses for any amount of time can tell you—it isn't *if* you're going to get hurt, it's *when*. I don't want that to sound worse than it is, because the truth is that most horse-related injuries boil down to nothing more than stepped-on toes or minor cuts and bruises, particularly when it comes to the average backyard horse owner. However, there's always the chance of more serious injuries, and I suppose there just isn't any way around that.

You see, anytime you put an animal as small, slow, and non-perceptive as a human next to an animal as big, fast, and highly perceptive as a horse, bad things are bound to happen . . . eventually. It's usually not the horse's fault (although we generally feel better if we can blame the horse), and it's usually not the human's fault. In truth, these are just things that happen.

It had been years since I'd suffered a major horse-related injury, perhaps fifteen or twenty years. In fact, I was very proud of the fact that I was able to stay injury-free for so long. Having worked with some pretty troubled horses during that time, I guess I felt like that was quite an accomplishment. Because things seemed to be going along so well, I think I got just a little complacent. I not only got a little lax in my work around horses, I wasn't doing anything to improve the work I was doing. After all, why fix what isn't broke?

But isn't it always the way? Just when you start to maybe get a little self-satisfied, reality jumps out of the bushes and gives you one big old slap on top of the head. And that's just what happened to me. Over about a three-year period, a series of events occurred that eventually brought me out of the contented little spot I was in concerning my horse work and threw me right into the deep end.

The first event came while I was managing the horse operation at a guest ranch up in the mountains. In a roundabout sort of way, we had ended up with a small Belgian draft horse by the name of Gus. Now, when I say small, you need to realize that I'm speaking in relative terms. He stood about sixteen hands tall and weighed about 1,850 pounds. The other Belgians we had averaged seventeen-and-a-half hands tall and weighed in at about 2,100 pounds.

At any rate, Gus had been pretty badly abused over the years and was ultimately taken away from his previous owner by the State for that abuse. The owner had wrapped the horse's barrel in barbed wire and tied a rope to the wire. Anytime he felt the horse did something wrong, he gave the rope a good jerk, tightening up the wire.

Well, needless to say, the owner was eventually reported, and the horse was confiscated and sold to a more caring owner. Unfortunately, because of the mental damage the horse had suffered, the new owner found he was a little too much to handle, and so Gus went up for sale again.

I was looking for another team of draft horses, due to our heavy schedule of hay rides in the summer and sleigh rides in the winter. At the time, we had two teams, but I wanted one more as a backup in case of injury and to make sure the other teams got some well-earned time off.

When I saw Gus for the first time, he was hitched to a beet wagon with his new partner, Woodrow. The owner was selling the pair dirt-cheap. Basically, what the deal boiled down to was that if I bought Woodrow, he would throw in Gus for free. Now Woodrow was more the size of our other Belgians, very well trained, and worked well in harness. I could see right off that he would fit right into our program.

Gus, however, was more of an unknown quantity. He was spooky, defensive, and really too small for what we needed him for. But the price for the team was real right. I watched Gus and Woodrow pull the old beet wagon around for a while and noticed that Gus seemed more than willing to work. In fact, despite his size, he not only pulled equally with the bigger horse, he often out-pulled him!

To make a long story short, I ended up buying the team and taking them back to the ranch. Within a week's time, we began working with them and found Woodrow to be very easy to get along with, a hard worker, and very friendly around people. Gus, on the other hand, was hard to catch and halter, worried a lot when he was tied, and preferred no one touch or pet him. He flinched and shook uncontrollably when we harnessed him or hooked him to the wagon, and he worried a lot when we tried to bridle him. Once he was hooked to the wagon, though, it was another story. He was responsive, hard working, and seemed very happy.

Over the next year or so, we used Gus and Woodrow primarily for chores around the ranch, feeding and hauling wood mostly. With Gus being as skittish as he was, we didn't want him coming in contact with the guests at the ranch for fear he might accidentally hurt someone. During that year, we handled him just like we did our other horses, with respect and dignity, and hoped that would be enough for him to start trusting us.

To some degree, our way of thinking worked. By the following summer Gus had quieted down around people enough that we were able to use him and Woodrow for some of the evening hay rides, as well as occasionally using them as the lead team in our four-up. He was allowing himself to be caught without any trouble, and harnessing was no longer a life-or-death situation for him. Bridling could still be a little touchy, but for the most part I was beginning to feel he was close to being out of the woods.

That all seemed to change one evening in July. We had just finished a hay ride with Gus and Woodrow, and everything had gone off without a hitch. On the way back to the barn, Gus started to get a little antsy. It was nothing major, and because we ended up doing this particular hay ride earlier in the day than usual, the team didn't get fed at their usual time. As a result, I just dismissed Gus's antsy behavior as him being hungry and ready for supper.

We parked the hayrack and unhooked the team, and I drove them over to the hitchrail to pull the harness off. I was being helped that evening by my head wrangler, Susie Heidi, and when I brought the team over, Susie was already there waiting for us. She was in charge of pulling Woodrow's harness; I was in charge of Gus's.

We had coiled the lines, and I was ready to take Gus's bridle off so I could replace it with his halter, which was hanging on the ten-inch diameter hitchrail in front of us. Susie would do the same with Woodrow. For some reason, this evening Gus was holding his head higher than normal when I started to take his bridle off. As a result, I ended up slightly underneath his head and just in front of his chest, as I reached up to remove the bridle.

I had no sooner slipped the bridle over his ears than, without any warning whatsoever, he lunged forward, pinning me between the heavy hitchrail and his massive chest. My arms had been up over my head while I was removing his bridle, so my exposed rib cage was jammed against the hitchrail. The air was forced out of my lungs so fast I never knew what hit me.

Whatever spooked Gus worried him so much that he continued to drive forward for a second or two, before he turned to his left and bolted for his nearby pen. As he went, he pretty effectively rolled my body down the hitchrail and deposited me on the ground just past its end.

After a second or two, I was back on my feet and heading toward Gus's pen, where he was frantically pacing, harness and all, in front of the closed gate. At first, I felt okay. I knew I'd been pinned against the rail and that my back hurt a little, but other than that, I didn't think I was hurt. That is, until I took about four or five steps forward. All at once, I couldn't breathe, and an excruciating pain shot through my lower back. The pain went all the way down into my lower right leg, and I could feel a burning sensation on the outside of my right calf.

I immediately dropped to my knees, unable to do anything. There was a pain in the left side of my rib cage that went up into my shoulder, and trying to hold myself up with my left hand made that shoulder hurt like nothing I'd felt before.

"Are you okay?" I could hear Susie ask.

I looked up at her and could see by the look on her face that I probably wasn't.

"Yeah," I struggled to get the words out. "See if you can get him tied up."

She went to Gus's pen and opened the gate, letting him into the pen, harness and all. She closed the gate and returned to where I was kneeling.

"I'd better get some help," she said, as she turned on her heel and ran for the main part of the ranch.

The accident had taken less than three seconds, but I would suffer the effects of it for years to come. In those three seconds, I cracked two ribs, separated my collarbone, and herniated two discs in my back. I also had a collapsed lung and a ruptured bursal sac in my right elbow.

It was safe to say my horse-related, serious-injury-free streak was officially over.

I soon found that having what turned out to be a chronic back problem changed things considerably for me when it came to the work I was doing. Riding or just being in the saddle had always been a very comfortable thing. I really enjoyed it and tried to spend as much time in the saddle as I could. After this accident, however, the saddle started to become a place I dreaded.

To start with, just getting in the saddle was difficult. When I mounted from the left side of the horse, I had trouble lifting my right leg high enough to clear the cantle. Getting on from the right side of the horse wasn't an option either, because I didn't have enough strength in my right leg to support my weight in the stirrup long enough to swing my left leg over. Once I was on the horse, I found it hard to find a spot where I could be physically comfortable for more than a couple of minutes. My lower back would spasm on the right side and my upper back would spasm on the left.

And that was pretty much how things went for the next nine months. After that, the pain and spasms seemed to taper off some, or maybe I just got used to them. Either way, riding had become a little more physically tolerable by the following spring.

The pain and discomfort in my back pretty much leveled off for the next couple of years. I still had days when things would flare up again, but luckily I had some painkillers the doctor gave me for those times. Overall, things weren't too bad, and over time, the pain did become easier to deal with on a daily basis.

About three years later, however, my physical "wheels" would fall off once and for all. It started when three apparently inconsequential events happened in succession. What I didn't know at the time was that these three events would send me into a tailspin it would take years to get out of.

I was riding a client's young horse, one I'd started a few weeks before, in a sixty-foot round pen. He was going well at the time, and I hadn't even planned to ride him that day. It's just that the weather was real nice, and we'd just put down some new footing in the pen. The colt was used to the more solid footing of trails and the big arena, so I wanted to see how he would do on a little softer surface.

I decided I'd only be on him for a half-hour or so, and for the first few minutes in the pen, he did just fine. But I soon found that not only was the new footing much softer than what he was used to, it was also applied very unevenly. One spot in particular went from about three inches in depth to well over nine or ten. That spot was where the trouble came.

We went through the deep spot on our first pass around the pen, and he seemed only a little nervous. But on the second pass, it was just too much for him to handle. He got to the middle of this ten-foot-wide, twelve-foot-long section of sand and started to flounder. He lunged forward, stopped, and tried to jump straight up. As soon as he landed, he offered a half-hearted buck and then suddenly reared straight up in the air. That's what got me.

As he rose, he threw his head up with such force it hit me smack on the jaw, the leather of his headstall splitting my chin wide open. (I would later find my hat thirty feet away on the other side of the round-pen fence!) I stayed on him until he went up so high I felt he would go over backward, and at that point I let myself fall. I landed in the soft sand and looked up to see him teetering in midair on his hind legs.

Thinking he was going to fall over on top of me, I instinctively started scrambling on my hands and knees toward the fence, but my efforts were to no avail. The sand was so deep I couldn't move. I stopped scrambling and braced myself for the crash I was sure would come, but much to my surprise, it didn't. I looked up to see the gelding regain his balance and fall off to the side, landing on all fours. He scrambled out of the deep sand and took off for the other side of the pen.

Other than the fact that my chin was bleeding from an inch-long gash, the incident left me no worse for wear. Or so I thought. On my way home later that day, my back began to bother me again; within a couple of days I was having trouble getting out of bed and walking.

About a month later I was riding my horse, Buck, bringing our herd of about seventy-five saddle horses in off the pasture. It was the spring of the year, and after a winter of unusually heavy snowfall, we'd had an unusually large amount of rain. The ground was not only saturated, there were springs coming up all over the ranch in places we never knew springs existed.

We gathered the horses up without any trouble and took them into the forty-foot-wide, quarter-mile-long chute that led from the pasture to the big catch pen up near the barn. About halfway between the pasture and the barn, the chute made a ninety-degree turn.

We had a few new horses in the herd, and this was their first time being gathered this way. Buck and I brought the horses through the chute, made the ninety-degree turn, and headed for the open gate of the catch pen. We almost had the entire bunch through the gate when two of the new horses turned and bolted back toward the pasture.

Immediately, Buck and I turned and raced back toward where the chute made the turn. Back then, Buck was so fast it was hard for any horse to get past him, but these two were giving it their best. Still, we got out ahead of them without any trouble and worked our way toward pinning them against the rail so we could turn them back.

Suddenly, without any apparent reason, Buck started to slow. Thinking the horses might get past us, I urged him forward. But just as I did, he decided to hit the brakes—hard. He did a perfect reining-horse slide on his back end for just a few feet before his front end just dropped out from under him. He jolted to a stop, and I was catapulted over his head. I did a somersault in the air and landed spread-eagle on my back in the mud. It turns out we had hit a newly developed sinkhole in the middle of the chute, one of many that had sprouted up all over the ranch. Buck was fine, but my back injury was once again aggravated by the fall.

Just three weeks later, before my body had time to heal from the sinkhole episode, I was in the big arena riding a liver-chestnut mare named Cinder. We had been working for about forty-five minutes and were just getting ready to finish up, when I decided to lope her one more lap. We got about halfway around the arena in a nice, easy lope when Cinder stumbled. At first I figured she would just pick herself up and finish the circle, but it quickly became evident that wasn't going to happen.

Within just a few feet, she lost her balance to the point where her nose hit the dirt in front of her. Once that happened, her face and head started to roll under her and her back end began to lift off the ground. I felt as though she was about to flip over, so I decided it might not be such a bad time to get off. I just sort of made a dive for it, landing off to the side in the sand of the arena. I did an almost flawless execution of a tuck and roll as I hit the ground and was on my feet almost immediately.

As it turned out, Cinder didn't flip after all, but she did skin up her nose pretty badly. I was standing there looking at her as she climbed to her feet, thinking I felt pretty good, considering that was my third fall in less than three months. Then I took a step. A pain seared through the left side of my lower back as if I'd been shot.

Dang it, I thought to myself in disgust. *I screwed my back up AGAIN!*

This time I had actually broken a bone in my back and bruised a kidney. I couldn't believe it; I hadn't been on the ground for more than a couple of seconds. But I guess, sometimes, a couple of seconds is all the time it takes.

It wasn't long before I realized that every time I got off a horse, my whole body hurt. My ankles, knees, hips, lower back, shoulders, and neck all ached. It was a weird feeling, because in the past, not only did my body not hurt after riding, it actually felt good. At the time, I told myself the pain was nothing more than a by-product of all my back problems. I brushed it off and went about my business.

A year or so later, however, one of my wranglers showed me a picture she'd taken of me riding Buck in the arena. At first I couldn't believe it was even me, and I actually had to look twice to make sure it was. Granted, it had been years since I'd seen a picture of myself in the saddle, but what I saw in that photo took me completely by surprise.

There I was, sitting in the saddle, hunched over from the waist, my legs thrust forward in the stirrups with my knees almost locked and my backside pushed tight up against the back of the saddle seat. In short, I was one big brace from the bottom of my feet to the top of my head. More than likely, that was the source of the soreness I felt throughout my body every time I got off a horse.

It was in complete contrast to a photo I'd seen of myself years before, loping a big black horse named Roulette across the yard of the ranch where I worked. Back then, my entire body—legs, seat, back . . . everything—was quiet and relaxed, and the two of us looked as if we were moving effortlessly together.

But this, I thought to myself. *How did I ever come to be riding like THIS?*

Well, the answer was pretty simple, although it was still quite some time before I got it figured out. I was riding that way because my back hurt. I was tightening all the muscles in my lower back in an effort to protect the injured area. By doing so, I was inadvertently throwing myself out of balance. The more I fought to regain my balance, the more out of balance I got and the more braced and protective my body became.

You see, what I didn't understand at the time is that our balance actually comes from our "center," a spot about two inches below the navel. When we bring awareness to our center, balance is easy, whether we're sitting, walking, running, riding a horse, or whatever we might be doing. When we're not aware of our center, we are easily thrown out of balance, so we try to find artificial or mechanical ways to regain or, for that matter, just maintain our balance. By the looks of that photo, that is exactly what I was doing . . . mechanically trying to stay in balance.

While the way I was riding in the photograph bothered me, I pretty much wrote it off as my new lot in life. The injuries were there, and they probably weren't going to get any better, so that was more than likely the way I was going to have to ride from there on out. That was that, I figured.

And besides, I convinced myself, as long I stayed on a horse when things went bad, what was the difference anyway? After all, I had been on plenty of jumpy horses since my injuries. Some of those horses even went to bucking pretty good, and I was still able to stay on. The ones I didn't stay with, well, those situations were out of my control anyway—my client's horse rearing in deep sand, Cinder falling on her nose, Buck hitting a sinkhole. In each case, it had been better that I didn't stay on. At least that's what I told myself.

Looking back, that way of thinking just made it easier for me to believe my riding wasn't really a problem, when in reality it was. Not only was this a problem for me, but it was also a problem for the horses I was riding. But I was still a ways away from being able to see that, too.

Something else about my horse work got my attention about the same time my riding skills began to deteriorate. It started when a little horse was brought to me for training. He was an extremely troubled Arabian that was so terrified of everything and everybody around him that he didn't look comfortable in his own skin. Since riding him was out of the question due to his high fear level, I decided to spend some time working with him on the ground.

I began in the round pen, thinking it would be a great place for him to work out his anxieties and learn I wasn't there to harm him. I figured maybe an hour of quiet work every day for three or four days would help him feel better, and before long, we'd be able to get on him. Well, three weeks later he wasn't any better than he had been on the first day. Three weeks after that, there still wasn't much change. Weeks turned into months and months turned into a year, and still there wasn't much improvement.

Everything I knew to do with a horse like this—everything that had always worked in the past—did not work with him. Not even close. It became painfully obvious to me this was a horse that was solidly stuck where he was in his life. He'd been there for a long time, and even though he was very uncomfortable in that place, he wasn't willing or able to change.

It was actually this little Arab that got me thinking harder about how I was doing things when it came to my work with horses. After over a year of not seeing much progress, I slowly began to realize that maybe it wasn't just him that was stuck where he was.

The good news about the little Arabian is that a solution finally came to me. It took a total of about fourteen months. However, once we had our breakthrough, things progressed pretty nicely. The solution, not surprisingly, was actually very simple.

All along I made sure to ease around him at all times. Basically I'd been tiptoeing around every time I came in contact with him, almost to the point of babying him. My goal in doing so was to show him I wasn't interested in hurting him. With a lot of troubled horses, this way of handling them is very effective, but it obviously wasn't for this one. In fact, I kept getting the feeling that my quiet behavior made him even more nervous than he already was, which I just couldn't figure out.

But one day I began to try to look at the situation more from his point of view. I asked myself how I would feel if people tiptoed around me all the time. I decided it would probably make me a little nervous. I would constantly be wondering what was wrong or why they were treating me that way, especially if I didn't feel there was a reason for it. I began to wonder if that was how the little Arab felt.

All that time, my behavior toward him had been an attempt to be comforting. What if he didn't see it that way? What if he actually saw it as the complete opposite? If that were the case, he was probably looking at me with more suspicion than confidence.

After coming to this realization, I went out the next day and proceeded to go about my business with him, just as if he were any other horse, which, it turned out, is exactly what he was. I entered his pen with the intent of haltering him. Usually this would be at least a five-minute ordeal, with me easing up to him, then him spinning, running, side passing, backing, turning, putting his nose in the corner of the pen, and finally standing there shaking, as I gingerly slipped his halter on.

On this day I went into the pen and walked right up to him—no hesitation, no fooling around. Surprisingly, he stood right there. He did suck back a little and act as though he was going to move, but he never did. I put his halter on him at the same speed I would any other horse, and he never budged. I led him out of the pen and down to the round pen, kindly but firmly communicating, "This is where we're going, and this is how fast we're going there." For the first time since he arrived, he walked the 200 yards to the round pen without spooking or trying to pull away from me.

In the round pen, I asked him to do everything using the same kind of intent, basically saying to him, "This is what I'm looking for and here's how I want you to try to do it." He was able to perform everything I asked of him flawlessly without much worry at all. On the way back to his pen, he walked quietly with his head down, something I had never seen him do. He still struggled a little over the next several days, but within about ten days, he was quiet enough to saddle. A couple of days later we were up and riding him. I couldn't believe how little it took to get a change from him, and even more importantly, I couldn't believe how long it took to find the solution. I guess an argument can be made that during the four-teen months prior to the horse's change, I was laying the ground-work for him to come through, and I suppose that's true. But I have to wonder how long he might have been asking me to try something different in my approach, and I just didn't catch it.

It was pretty clear to me that I had not only missed something in the way I was trying to communicate to this horse, I had also missed something in the way he was trying to communicate back. As a re-sult, I began to question just about everything I was doing with horses and even what I believed to be true regarding the philosophy behind what I was doing.

I must say, it didn't take me long to find some discrepancies. For instance, there is a longstanding doctrine that in order to get a horse to do what you want, you simply make the wrong thing difficult and the right thing easy. As I thought things through, I wasn't sure even that way of thinking held water.

Let's look at a horse that doesn't want to be caught. Generally we put the horse in a round pen and chase him until he decides to stand still. In other words, we make the wrong thing (not standing still) difficult by urging the horse to move more than he'd like. When he does the correct thing (stand still), we remove the pressure to keep moving. The wrong thing—moving—is difficult; the right thing—standing still—is easy. It's a simple concept, and frankly, it can be very effective. But is there another way?

If we look at this example another way, isn't the wrong thing in this particular case already difficult for the horse? I mean, we want him to stand still; he mentally struggles with that, so he moves. By definition, the act of moving is physically harder than standing still, so in a sense, the horse is already making it harder on himself. Now both things are difficult. One is mentally difficult; the other is physically difficult. If both these things are hard for the horse, why do we want to make either one harder? That seems counterproductive.

I began wondering what would happen if we made both options easy for the horse, instead of making either option harder. Would there even be a way to do that? If both options were easy for the horse, would it then be easier for us to direct him to the option we want him to choose, or would he remain difficult to catch?

These are just a few of the many questions I began to ask myself following the injuries I sustained and after working with the little Arab horse. I was beginning to realize something had to change in the way I was thinking about my work and performing it. But admittedly, I lacked the proper motivation to look. And a more slippery slope than that, one might never find.

But life was already beginning to prod me in a direction that would give me more than enough incentive to improve my work. And once I was on that path, it didn't take long for me to realize I would have to do more than just go along for the ride, if I was to come through to the other side.

4

A Full Cup

There was once a warrior who spent his life studying martial arts. He traveled all over the world searching out the best teachers and instructors, learning all they had to teach. In each dojo, he would learn a new discipline. Then he diligently studied the moves, nuances, and techniques day-in and day-out, for hours and hours, until he had them all down perfectly, before he moved on to the next instructor and the next new discipline.

The warrior had a tremendous amount of natural ability, and because of this, learning came very easy for him. Many of the teachers he worked with couldn't believe the speed at which he mastered even the most difficult of moves and techniques. In many cases, the warrior's knowledge and skill surpassed that of the instructor in only a matter of weeks.

The warrior's goal was to one day be able to study with the Grand Master, a wise old man whose ability and knowledge were unsurpassed by anyone on earth. But the warrior didn't just want to be able to study with the Grand Master; he wanted to be the best, most knowledgeable student the Grand Master had ever had. So he continued his search for knowledge and skill.

Years passed and when he had the knowledge and skill he thought would impress the Grand Master, the warrior finally began his trek to the Master's village. The old Master lived way back up in the mountains, and it took the warrior nearly a year to reach the small, remote village. The Master's humble dwelling sat in a clearing at the edge of town, and it was his wife who came to the door when the warrior respectfully knocked.

"I have come a very long way," the warrior said, as he bowed. "I hope to have a word with the Grand Master."

"Of course," the old woman replied politely. "Come in."

The warrior followed the woman into the small but well-kept house. She motioned for him to sit, which he did with a respectful bow.

"I will tell him you are here," she said with a smile, as she disappeared into another room, sliding the door closed behind her.

The warrior could hardly contain himself. After all those years of training, all those years of traveling, he was finally here, in the home of the Grand Master. In just a few short minutes, he would meet him face to face. He hoped his excitement wouldn't be too evident.

He sat patiently for several minutes, but neither the Master nor his wife came from the room. Several more minutes passed and still nobody came out. Minutes turned into an hour, then an hour became two, then three, then four. The warrior began to fidget. Two more hours passed before the Master's wife emerged from the room. She smiled and nodded as she walked past the warrior.

"Excuse me, madam," the warrior said. "Does he know I'm still here?"

"He does," she replied, as she walked out the front door.

The warrior's patience began to dwindle. Another hour passed. The warrior was beginning to feel a little put out. After all, he had just spent the majority of his life training specifically so that he could be good enough to study with the Grand Master. He had traveled a year just to find this village. And now, the Master was making him wait for what seemed an eternity.

The warrior rose from his seat and began slowly pacing the floor. Another hour passed. The warrior quietly cleared his throat. He paced some more and cleared his throat a little louder. One more hour passed; he coughed loudly. Another hour passed. The warrior was, by this time, beside himself. He had just about decided that he'd waited long enough and was about to leave when the door to the back room slowly slid open.

There, on the other side of the door, was a small, gray-bearded man with kind eyes. It was the Grand Master at last. He slowly motioned for the warrior to follow him.

The Master motioned for the warrior to take a seat across from him at a small table in the middle of the room. On the table were two teacups and a pot of tea. The warrior impatiently sat down.

"Tea?" the master asked.

"Yes, thank you," the warrior replied. "I'm a bit thirsty. I've been waiting a long time with nothing to eat or drink."

The Master nodded as he slowly poured some tea into the warrior's cup. Without hesitation, the warrior began to list his accomplishments in the world of martial arts. The old man, listening intently, began to pour tea slowly into his own cup.

The warrior's list was a long one—the battles he had fought and won, the disciplines he had followed, and the teachers he had studied with. The Master continued to pour as he listened. Soon, his cup was full and the tea was running over the top of the cup and onto the saucer. The warrior noticed this somewhat odd behavior, but kept talking anyway, wanting to get it all out before the Master asked him to stop.

The warrior spoke of all the countries he'd been to and the oceans he had sailed to get there. Still the master poured, and tea was now running all over the table. Finally, the warrior stopped.

"Excuse me, Master," the warrior said, almost apologetically. "Your cup is full."

"Yes," the Master replied quietly. "And you are very much like this cup. You are so full, nothing more can go in." The Master stopped pouring and gently placed the teapot on the table. "I will not be able to teach you anything, until you empty something from your cup."

"But Master," the warrior said, taken aback. "Everything I've learned so far has been useful in some way. Tell me, what should I empty out of my cup in order to learn from you?"

"That is not for me to decide," the Master said quietly. "It is your cup, not mine."

❁

As I said before, I led a pretty sheltered life when it comes to my work with horses. I suppose that's why it was such a complete surprise to me when the pieces all fell into place in the mid-1990s and I began to do formal training clinics on a full-time basis. Who would have ever thought?

The first several clinics were relatively small, with a half-dozen or so riders and a handful of auditors. The format was relatively simple. I'd work with one horse and one rider at a time for an hour or so each day over a period of two to four days. I tried very hard to stick to the three main principles I learned as a kid and had carried on to adulthood—always work with the horse, not against him; always listen to what the horse is trying to say; and most importantly, try hard to think for yourself. (These days, I believe some folks refer to this as thinking outside the box.)

The people who attended my early clinics as riders, as well as the auditors who showed up, all seemed genuinely interested in what we were doing with the horses, and there were even a few questions asked by the folks who had come to watch. Most people seemed interested in the work itself. Their questions were geared toward why or how the things we were doing with the horses worked (or, in some cases, didn't work).

These kinds of questions often sparked great conversations between the riders, the auditors, and myself that sometimes went on for quite a while. Just about every time this happened, it seemed to generate (and this may sound sort of silly) a general feeling of togetherness. It was as if we were all in this thing together, all searching for something that would ultimately benefit the horse.Overall, it was a great way to get my feet wet, and I felt pretty good about how those first several clinics went.

But as time went on, things changed. As the clinics began to get bigger and more folks came to watch, I noticed a shift in the tone and subject of the questions that were asked. I began getting questions from folks that didn't really seem to have a whole lot of bearing on anything we were doing. These questions almost never came from the riders. They always seemed to come from auditors who were often only at the clinic for one day or, in many cases, just part of a day.

There was one clinic in particular, relatively early on, where we had just finished up all the horses for the morning and were getting ready to break for lunch. I was still standing inside the round pen, and I asked if there were any other questions before we went to lunch.

"I've got one," a lady in a big-brimmed hat said. "I noticed you only use the flat, web halters when you work."

"Yes, that's right," I replied.

"How come?" she asked.

At first I thought it was a trick question or maybe even some kind of joke. After all, what possible difference did it make what kind of halter I used? But the look on her face told me her question was indeed serious.

"Well," I explained, "they're the kind of halters I grew up using. Actually, the ones I grew up with were leather, but the nylon ones seem to hold up a little better and take less maintenance."

"So you feel the web halters are better than the rope ones?"

"I didn't say that," I smiled. "I said they were what I grew up using."

"But aren't rope halters safer?" She got up from her chair and walked to the round-pen fence. "The metal hardware on those nylon halters can break, if a horse pulls back hard enough."

"Anything can break if a horse pulls back hard enough," I shrugged.

"Not a rope halter," she argued.

I could see this was going nowhere fast, so I decided to try to get out of it as gracefully as I could.

"Well, like I said, they're what I grew up using . . ."

"Don't you think a halter that doesn't break when a horse pulls back is safer than one that does?" she interrupted.

"I guess it would depend on the situation," I said matter-of-factly. "If a horse fights so hard when he pulls back that he could break his neck, then I guess I'd prefer the halter break before his neck does."

"But if he learns he can get away by breaking the halter, won't that just teach the horse to pull back?"

"It seems to me," I said, "if he breaks the halter when he pulls back, he already knows how to pull back."

Several people chuckled, which sort of forced the woman to smile a little.

"Oh, you know what I mean," she said, as if I actually did.

I shrugged again.

"It's just that I was a little surprised," she interjected. "Every other clinician I've seen is using the rope ones."

"Maybe one day I will too," I conceded. "But for now, I just use what I'm comfortable with."

This type of exchange actually got to be pretty common at the clinics for a while. The subject matter often changed, but the bottom line usually didn't. People wanted to know why I wasn't doing the same things, saying the same things, or using the same tools as all the other trainers out there doing clinics.

Well, the answer to that is simple. As I was growing up, I learned how to do things a little differently than the others. It wasn't that what I learned was better, and it wasn't that it was worse. It was just different . . . that's all. In the end, I believe we are all heading in the same direction. It's just that we are taking slightly different paths to get there.

Be that as it may, I must admit after a year or so of hearing those types of questions over and over, it started to get to me. So much so that I not only found myself behaving somewhat defensively when answering them, but each time one was posed to me, I began to question myself. Heck, what did I know anyway? I'd really only been exposed to one way of doing things all my life. What if what I was doing was wrong? I'd never know the difference!

So here's the paradox I was presented with. On one side of the coin, most of the riders I was working with at the clinics seemed very happy with the results they were getting with their horses. Word was beginning to spread about the kind of work we were doing, and as a result, we were getting lots of requests to do clinics, literally all over the world.

On the other side of the coin, I was having trouble with my own riding due to my injuries, and I had begun to question the philosophy behind some of the things I was doing in my horse work. On top of all that, people I didn't even know, in places all over the country, were questioning what I was doing and how I was doing it, for no other reason, it seemed, than it wasn't the way other trainers or clinicians were doing it.

Externally I was still able to operate at a pretty high level. Internally, however, I was beginning to become bogged down with worry and self-doubt. Now, don't get me wrong. I've always believed that questioning yourself from time to time is a good thing. It keeps you thinking and hopefully progressing. But if you question yourself to the point of stagnation, well, that can be a problem. And I believe that was exactly where I was heading.

In other words, my cup was filling up.

There was no question something needed to change, and lucky for me, that change was just right around the corner.

Eastern Tennessee is a beautiful place in the fall of the year. The trees are plumb full of fireflies at night, and the days are often sunny and warm. Not that sticky, almost unbearable heat they get down there in middle of the summer, but a comfortable, sleep-in-the-hammock-under-a-shade-tree kind of warmth. This was my third trip to eastern Tennessee, and it was one I always enjoyed making. My hosts were great. They were friendly, helpful people, and the clinic was always well run, with open and enthusiastic riders and auditors.

This particular clinic was a little bit different than most I had done, in that three of the people riding were men. Up until then, the vast majority of riders had been women. At any rate, the fourth rider of the day was one of these men, a fellow named Rick.

It was the first day of a four-day clinic and I'd only had a chance to visit with Rick briefly the night before, when I was introduced to all the riders. For that reason I didn't have a good feel for who Rick was or where he was in his horsemanship. My impressions were that he was quiet, down to earth, and very interested in what was going on at the clinic.

We began his session just like we do with pretty much everyone else. I asked several questions about his horse, a real nice little Paso mare he had mostly been using for trail riding and working cattle on his farm up in North Carolina. He told me he had been riding for quite some time and that he and his wife had several horses back home. However, he had been struggling with this particular horse.

I asked him to ride the mare around a little, so we could have a look. He stepped her off at a walk inside the big arena, and at first everything seemed just fine. Some issues began to show up pretty quickly though. It was clear the mare was very well trained, and she seemed willing. It's just that the longer the two went along together, the more they began looking like oil and water.

Rick would ask her to do something, and she would make an effort to comply, but because of incidental movement with his hands or legs or a shift of weight that he didn't need to make, he inadvertently got in her way. That caused her to be unable to do the task, which turned into a misunderstanding between them.

Because of this misunderstanding, Rick would almost unwittingly push the mare a little harder to perform the task. Confused about what he was asking, she would try something different. When he told her that what she was trying wasn't what he wanted, she would get mad. This cycle repeated itself over and over, until both Rick and the horse weren't having a whole lot of fun.

During the first half-hour of his session, I asked Rick to make a few small adjustments, but they didn't seem to help much. The picture between the two still looked skewed, and I couldn't seem to put my finger on the problem. All I knew for sure was they were working against one another, instead of with one another.

I asked Rick to bring the mare to a stop, so we could visit about what was going on. We talked briefly about how he was using his hands and seat, and then I mentioned something else.

"When I watch the two of you go," I said, "it looks like you're working against each other pretty much the whole time.

Keep in mind, as soon as she starts moving, she will automatically establish a rhythm. Your job will be to get in time with that rhythm. Let her movement move you instead of the other way around."

I paused at that point, expecting, I guess, some kind of acknowledgment of understanding from Rick. But instead he just sat quietly looking back at me.

"In other words," I continued, "once you put the cue on, she'll initiate the movement. All I want you to try to do is blend with that movement, then direct it to where you'd like it to go . . . not force it to where you want it to go."

Rick still didn't respond, but the look on his face told me I was losing him. It's been my experience that when I talk with certain riders about blending with movement, it's sometimes difficult for them to comprehend. In a case like that, the rider shuts down mentally, and it can take quite a bit to get them back on track. I hoped I hadn't done that with Rick.

"I know it sounds a little like Zen horseback riding," I said with a slight smile, "but we just want to make her job as easy for her as possible."

Still no response.

"Do you see what I mean?" I asked, in hopes I would get some kind of feedback telling me how far off target I might be.

"Yes," he replied quietly. "Let me give it a try."

And with that, they rode off.

Well, to say I was amazed at what happened next would be an understatement. Within a matter of seconds, all of the trouble Rick and the mare were having just seemed to melt away. For the next thirty minutes or so, the two of them went around that arena just as quiet and pretty as you please. They changed gaits and speeds within gaits virtually at will, with little or no visible cues, and their stops were quick and effortless.

When Rick's session was over, he rode up to me with a smile on his face.

"Well," I said, a bit surprised at what I had just seen, "I guess you did know what I meant by all that."

"I'll need to talk with you about this later," he said, dismounting. "If you have time."

"I will."

Later that evening I had the opportunity to sit down with Rick and his wife, Sandy, after supper. I had met Sandy the year before when I had been doing a clinic at the same place. She had attended as an auditor and was there now to watch Rick ride.

"Have you ever heard of a martial art known as aikido?" Rick asked, almost as soon as we sat down.

"No, I sure haven't."

"Well," he continued, "Sandy and I both teach aikido. It's a Japanese martial art. The word itself, aikido . . . ai-ki-do . . . translated, means 'the way of harmony.'"

"It's what you're teaching with your horsemanship," Sandy interjected.

"Yes," Rick continued. "The basic philosophy of aikido is to accept an attacker's energy, blend with it, then direct it, hopefully bringing the attack to a peaceful conclusion."

"I've never heard of it," I repeated.

For the next forty-five minutes or so, the three of us sat and discussed the many apparent similarities between working with horses and the martial art of aikido. Needless to say, the more we talked, the more interested I became. By the time we finished, Rick and Sandy had invited me up to their home in North Carolina. Sandy was hoping to get some help with one of her horses, but also the couple wanted to share some videos of aikido masters at work.

About a week later I was at their place. We worked with horses during the day and watched aikido videos in the evening. Rick explained that the primary difference between aikido and many of the other martial arts is that there are really no offensive moves in aikido. It is essentially a defensive art that uses the attacker's energy against him. In fact, the only way you can perform aikido effectively is to remain soft and quiet during the attack. In many other martial arts, force and overpowering the assailant are taught.

While I watched those videos, one of the things that struck me was how effortlessly the master was able to move and flow with his attackers' movements, no matter how many attackers he was faced with—in many cases six or seven at a time. The soft, flowing movement I was seeing was eerily reminiscent of what I'd seen when the old man rode his horses all those years ago!

By the time I left Rick and Sandy's place a couple of days later, I had a great interest in learning more about aikido and the possible practical applications it might have in the world of horsemanship. They had given me a list of books to read, a couple of videos to take home and watch, and a list of aikido dojos in Colorado, in case I wanted to check them out in person.

On a number of occasions during my stay, both Rick and Sandy suggested I might want to take up aikido as a way to improve my horse work. I told them it was probably a good idea and the first chance I got, I would look into it. In the back of my mind, though, something told me trying to take up a martial art in my shabby physical condition and at my age (over forty) might not be the smartest thing I could do.

However, learning more about the philosophy of the art and trying to implement that into my work was certainly something I could, and would, do. When I returned home, I ordered the books Rick and Sandy had suggested and read them from cover to cover as soon as they arrived. Some of the philosophies and ideas in the books were relatively easy to understand, while others were a little beyond my grasp at the time.

What little I did understand from the books, I tried to implement into my work right away. To be honest, trying to learn any skill from a book is a lot like trying to develop a long-term relationship with someone without actually meeting that person face to face. It can be done, but until you actually sit across from that person at a dinner table, you'll never know what they look like when they eat.

The truth of the matter is, I just wasn't able to take in a whole lot of new information right then anyway. You see, my cup was already full. I was worrying about the deterioration of my riding skills; I was worrying about things that others were saying about my work;

I was even questioning some of my own long-term beliefs about horsemanship. In other words, I was so bogged down with things that weren't relevant to where I wanted to be, nothing else could possibly go in. I just couldn't see that before I could learn anything new, something old and useless first needed to go.

Lucky for me, this was actually my long-awaited wake-up call. The only trouble was, I would need to go all the way to England before I was finally able to sit up and take notice of it.

5

The Fall

I'd done more flying in a few months than I had the entire rest of my life. Of course, that really isn't saying much, seeing as how the only other time I'd been in an airplane was about twenty years before. Even then I didn't get to land in it.

I was about twenty-two, when I ran into a group of friends I hadn't seen in a long time. We ended up in a bar, had a few beers, and decided to head up to this small airstrip the following day where, for $50, they would teach just about anybody the basics of how to properly jump out of an airplane (using a parachute, of course). For some reason, we were all unusually brave the night we merrily agreed to go, and I have to admit it did sound like a good idea at the time.

The next day, however, I don't think any of us were too sure we wanted to go through with it. At the same time, none of us wanted to be the first to chicken out, either. So, there we all were, listening to an ex-army ranger describe all the bad things that could go wrong when jumping out of a perfectly good airplane, not the least of which was hitting the ground at 200 miles per hour should your chute fail to open. After that, we spent time jumping off a variety of platforms and learning how to tuck and roll, so we didn't break either our legs (which evidently happened a lot, according to our instructor) or our heads.

Eventually, we learned what to do in an emergency should our primary chute fail to open. Finally, they put us all in WWII surplus jumpsuits and parachute harnesses, complete with parachutes, stuck us all in a little single-engine plane, took us up to 3,000 feet, and one by one kicked us out of the plane.

This was before the days of tandem jumps, where you basically strap yourself to the chest of an experienced jumper whose job it is to get you to the ground safely. No, we jumped by ourselves. The chutes were opened by static lines attached to our parachutes and connected to the plane. As we began falling helplessly to the earth, the line automatically snapped the chutes open for us.

Luckily for us, all our chutes opened just the way they should, and we all floated aimlessly back to the ground, none the worse for wear. Each of us got a swell T-shirt proclaiming we survived this perilous activity. Then we all went our separate ways and never saw each other again.

That had been my one and only time in an airplane. Now I'd flown a number of times in just the last few months. In September, I flew to Holland to do a couple of clinics, then to England for a couple more, and then back to Holland for another one before flying back home. In January, I flew from Denver to L.A. and then to Melbourne, Australia for a couple of clinics. When those were over, I flew from Melbourne to Adelaide for more clinics and then from Adelaide to Sydney for two more.

Spending all that time in airplanes had done nothing to help my ever-increasing backache, and by the time I got to Sydney, it was killing me. The clinic host picked me up at the airport and took me to her house, where I would spend two days resting before she drove me to the clinic venue about seventy miles away. Her young son helped bring my bags into the house, and as we entered the front door, I felt a strange twinge in the small of my back.

"Let us show you to your room," my hostess said with a smile. With that, she and her son walked quickly up the stairs to the second floor. I turned to close the front door, and without warning, my entire back seized up. The pain was like nothing I had felt before— it literally dropped me to my knees.

"Your room is right here," I could hear a faint voice say from upstairs. They must have thought I was right behind them when they climbed the stairs.

"Mark?" The voice was louder. "Are you coming?"

"In a minute," I answered in a voice with no air behind it.

I tried to crawl to the bag that contained my pain medication. It was only four feet away, but it seemed like a mile. As I tried to move, the pain in my back went through the roof, and this time it left me flat out on the floor.

"Oh, my," I heard my hostess say from the top of the stairs. "Are you all right?"

Her son was the first one to reach me.

"What's wrong?" he asked, with true concern in his voice.

"In that bag right there," I grunted. "Inside that bag is a smaller bag. Inside that small bag is a little orange bottle with some pills in it. Could you get it out and give me two of the pills, please?"

"Of course," he said, and he did.

My back was in a full-blown spasm, from my backside all the way up to my neck. The medication I took dulled the pain, but the spasm didn't release much. The next day I wasn't much better. One of the riders in the upcoming clinic was a massage therapist, and she offered to try to work the spasm out for me, which I reluctantly agreed to.

After nearly two-and-a-half-hours on her table, she miraculously got the spasm to subside. She later told me that it was one of the worst she'd seen. The muscles in my back were still plenty sore afterward, but at least I could work. The next day we drove the seventy miles and went ahead with the two clinics.

When we were finished, we drove back to Sydney, and I got on a plane headed for one more clinic at Grafton, then took another plane to Sydney, and another back to L.A. From there, I finally flew home to Colorado. Before I got home, I began experiencing what I described as low-grade flu symptoms. I was dizzy much of the time, so much so that putting my boots on sometimes caused me to fall over. I got sick to my stomach out of the blue, and I was getting carsick on a regular basis, sometimes even when I was driving. I would suddenly break out in a fever for a few hours and then it would go away. Some days were better than others, and while the symptoms were a nuisance, they were never really bad enough to keep me from working.

During February, I went to Alabama and Texas for a couple of clinics. Then in March I jumped on another airplane and flew to England and then up to Scotland for a couple of clinics. The symptoms came and went while I was in Scotland, with the worst flare-up coming during a car tour of the Scottish highlands. Imagine riding 200 miles on the wrong side of the road, sitting in the passenger seat (also on the wrong side) of a small car, on narrow roads with hundreds of twists, turns, and hills, while feeling like you have the flu.

At any rate, we finished up the clinics in Scotland, and I flew to England for a clinic there.

I am a firm believer that when something isn't going correctly between a person and a horse, the horse will do everything he can to show the person a better way of doing it. If we don't make a change in our behavior, the horse will perhaps protest in some way until we start trying to listen to what he has to say. If we still don't listen, the horse may escalate certain behavior to the point where it becomes undesirable. If we continue to ignore the fact that there's a problem, the behavior may go from being undesirable to downright dangerous. At that point, the person usually has no choice but to pay attention and begin to seek out a way to change the situation.

Over the years, I've come to understand that life does the same thing with us. When life isn't going well, situations or events just sort of present themselves to motivate us to make a decision about what to do to correct it. When we don't listen, these events might start to become undesirable little "hitches," if you will, that interrupt the flow of life. If we continue to ignore the fact that there's a problem, these events might turn from simply undesirable to dangerous.

My guess is that almost everyone can think of a time where things just weren't going right. Still, you probably kept going along like nothing was wrong and eventually a whole bunch of things started going bad. Yet, when you go back and fix the thing that initially wasn't right, everything else falls back into place and life not only resumes in a more positive way, it begins to flourish.

I believe I was at that crisis point by the time I flew to England. For years, things had been slowly unraveling for me, both physically and philosophically, yet I kept pushing forward like nothing was wrong. In the meantime, life had been nudging me along, trying to persuade me to make a change. I guess life had had enough of me dragging my feet.

The third rider of the day was a small woman on a great big, bay horse. This gelding was at least seventeen hands and easily weighed 1,200 pounds. He was five years old and came into the indoor arena looking like he was on pins and needles. The rider introduced herself with a smile, and when I asked what she wanted to work on, she told me flatly that her horse was afraid of tractors and she wanted to get him over it.

Seeing as how we were in an indoor arena with no tractors in sight, I wasn't real sure how we were going to accomplish that. So I asked a few questions about her and the horse to get a little background and found out the horse had been started under saddle less than a year before. Since that time, she had mostly taken him out for "hacks" (trail rides) and hadn't done much formal training with him.

I asked her to ride him around the arena, so I could have a look at the two of them together. I quickly saw he wasn't able to turn very well, didn't stop or back up, and was stiff as a board from nose to tail anytime he did move. When I asked her if what I was seeing was normal for him, she confirmed that it was.

I decided the best way to go in this case was to work on the basics, getting a stop with light pressure, getting turns with some softness, and getting him to back up properly. I figured once we got him softened up a little, he might feel better about being ridden in general, and hopefully that would eliminate some of his fears on the trail, especially when it came to tractors. After all, it seemed apparent he wasn't comfortable being ridden simply because he didn't know how to respond to any of the cues he was given. I figured if we explained to him what his job was, then he would be able to perform it better, and in turn, maybe he wouldn't worry so much.

He and his rider were only going to be at the clinic for two days during the four-day clinic, and the first day went pretty well. By the time their session was over, the big horse was stopping a little better and could turn with a little more softness. He couldn't back up as well as we wanted yet, but we would work on that a little more the next day.

On the second day of the clinic, my flu symptoms flared up again. I was a little dizzy as soon as I woke up, and I started feeling nauseous right after breakfast. Luckily the sick-to-my-stomach feeling subsided quite a bit by the time the clinic started. Even though I remained dizzy, the morning went along pretty uneventfully.

I worked with the rider and her big horse right after lunch, and we picked up where we left off the day before. The horse seemed much more settled than he had been the previous day, although there was still a bit of an edge to him, and by the time their session was over an hour-and-a-half later, I was actually feeling pretty good about how far the two of them had come. The horse's turns and stops looked much better, he could back up with relatively light pressure, and we even had an opportunity to start working on some transitions. At the end of the session, I asked the rider if there was anything else I could help her with.

"Well, actually, there is," she smiled from the back of her huge horse. "I was wondering if you wouldn't mind riding him for me. I've never seen anyone else on him, and I'd like to see how he goes."

"Sure," I said happily.

The problem was the horse was so big I couldn't even get my foot high enough to reach the stirrup, so someone brought in a chair for me to stand on so I could mount. The horse shied from the chair, and I made a small joke about him possibly being afraid of more than just tractors, which brought a chuckle from the crowd.

I spent a little time getting the horse used to standing beside the chair, which he was able to do relatively quickly. My legs were nearly twice the length of the owner's legs, so I adjusted the stirrups, climbed up on the chair, put my foot in the stirrup, and swung aboard. The English saddle was far too small for me, and the stirrups were still a little too short, even though they were let out as far as they could go. I figured I wasn't going to be on him all that long anyway, so what the heck . . .

Much to my surprise, as soon as I got into the saddle, I felt the big horse's back tighten, and he slowly bowed up as if he was getting ready to buck. Without hesitation I gently urged him forward, hoping it would be enough to change his mind, and almost right away the hump in his back went away. However, I was quickly faced with another little issue I hadn't thought of before I got on. We had only taken a few steps when I was hit with a wave of nausea and my dizziness suddenly intensified.

I took a few deep breaths, which helped some, but not much, and decided right then and there that I wouldn't ride the horse for very long. We did a few little transitions and changed speeds within the gait, but I couldn't help feeling as though the horse was tight and uncomfortable with me on his back.

Hang in there for a couple more minutes, big horse, I thought to myself. *We'll be done here pretty quick.*

After a few laps I felt it was probably time to get off, both for my sake and the sake of the horse. However, the cues I had been giving to the horse to achieve our transitions had been pretty subtle, and some of the auditors told me they couldn't see what I was doing. Almost as an afterthought, I invited several of them into the arena so they could get a closer look at what I was doing. Within a couple of seconds, ten or twelve auditors, in addition to the horse's owner, were standing in the middle of the arena watching as the horse and I made a few more laps around them.

I slightly exaggerated the cues I was using for the transitions and changes of speed, and within a couple of laps, most of the folks in the arena said they could now see what I was doing. That having been accomplished, we stopped facing the small group, and I pulled my right foot from the stirrup in order to get off. As I did, he let out a low grunt, bogged his head, and suddenly just went to bucking.

The bucking movement of this horse made me flash back to something that happened when I was a kid. The old man and I had gone to a little ranch on the other side of town to pick up a truck-load of hay. While we were there, a group of guys in a big arena were riding bulls. We sat and watched for a while, when out of the blue, the old man asked if I wanted to give it a try.

The bulls were relatively young, most being long yearlings or two-year-olds, and the majority seemed fairly cumbersome and slow, so I decided it might be fun. With some brief instruction from a guy named Don, who smelled a lot like the bulls themselves and who was down to two teeth on the top and one on the bottom, I tentatively climbed over the chute and down onto a bull's back.

Just sitting on his back in the chute, I got the feeling I had made a mistake by agreeing to this. The power in the little bull, even while he was just standing still, was like nothing I had felt before, and sitting there looking across the top of those broad, flat shoulders sort of made my mouth go dry and my palms begin to sweat. By this time, I had already been on a number of bucking horses and so I thought I knew what to expect. But when the door to the chute swung open and we were let out into that arena, I quickly found I wasn't as prepared as I thought I was.

The power of the bull was massive, and I had absolutely no control over his direction. At least with the bucking horses I had been on, I always had some control over the direction we were going. But I was completely at the mercy of that bull.

That was exactly how I felt when the big bay horse went to bucking. There was a tremendous amount of power, and I had no control over the horse's direction whatsoever. He bucked in a large circle around the people who were bunched up in the middle of the arena, turned back a couple times, ended up in a little trot, then slowed to a walk, and finally stopped.

Somewhere along the line I had slipped my foot back into the right stirrup, and after the horse stopped, I petted him for a couple seconds and then once again took my foot out of the stirrup in an effort to dismount. Again, the horse grunted and went back to bucking.

This scenario played itself out three more times over the next few minutes. The horse would stop, I'd try to get off, and he'd go to bucking. The good news was, he wasn't all that hard to ride when he was bucking. It was a sort of long, rolling buck with a pretty nice rhythm to it, and I was able to ride it relatively easily. The problem was that every time the horse stopped moving, I felt more and more sick to my stomach.

I knew I needed to get off that horse very soon, but I wasn't willing to just bail off him, whether he was moving or standing still. I really wanted him to let me get off, instead of just jumping off. Over time it began to look more and more like that wasn't going to happen, so I decided I was going to have to change things up if I was going to survive. My new plan was to try to put him in a straight line as much as I could the next time he broke loose and then see if I could get him to run instead of buck. If I could get him running, he'd hopefully only make a few laps before playing out, and we could put a stop to this foolishness once and for all.

We had once again come to a stop and, just like all the other times, I slipped my foot out of the stirrup and tried to get off. Once again he went to jumping and bucking. As planned, I sort of worked him into a straight line that went diagonally past the auditors who were still standing in a group in the middle of the arena. We were then heading toward the far right-hand corner of the arena. The big horse did even out and start running, as opposed to bucking, and as a result he covered the ground from the middle of the arena to the corner pretty quickly.

Okay, I said to myself. *All we need to do is make this turn and we're home free.*

Unfortunately, after riding through this horse's bucking fits for nearly five minutes, doing something as easy as making a little left turn actually proved to be the hard part. As we came flying into the corner, I picked up the left rein in an attempt to get him around the turn, and much to my surprise, he hit the brakes about as hard as he could. I unceremoniously flew off over his right shoulder and hit the wall of the arena with the force of a wrecking ball knocking down a brick wall. The problem was, in this case, the wall was still standing after the impact, and I was lying there in a heap in the dirt.

Looking back, that was probably an appropriate place for me to be. You see, before you can truly start to work your way back up out of a hole, you must first hit rock bottom. And on that day, I had hit bottom in more ways than one.

That fall was extremely hard for me to take for a couple of reasons. One was the fact that I just didn't come off horses very often. The simple fact that I hit the ground at all was somewhat of a shock to me. The last time I came off any horse was when Cinder nearly fell with me way back when, and I knew I hadn't come off a bucking horse in over thirty years! In fact, I stayed on *this* horse when he was bucking; I only came off him when he stopped. That was very disturbing for me. Heck, I could ride any horse while it was bucking, but couldn't seem to stay on one that was standing still!

From a physical standpoint, my body had taken yet another major hit. I had separated five ribs on my left side in the fall and that pain lingered for months. Finally, in July, four months after the fall, I went to the doctor to see if there was something I could do to ease the pain and was told there really wasn't. While I was there, I also mentioned to the doctor the flu symptoms I was still having and found out I'd been battling an inner-ear infection, probably since my return from Australia back in January. It was the infection that was causing me to be dizzy and have trouble with my balance, among other things.

At first, that actually seemed like good news for me, because I readily blamed my balance issues (and therefore my fall) on the inner-ear infection. I tried to convince myself maybe I wasn't riding that badly after all. But in reality, the time for excuses was over and somehow I knew it. Something needed to change.

I stumbled through the rest of the clinic season, taking medication for my inner-ear problem and nursing my injured ribs and lower back. By the time November rolled around and my clinic schedule for the year was finished, I was ready to sit down and have a good, long talk with myself about the way things were going.

I made a mental list of all the things I thought were going well and all the things I thought weren't going well. On the upside, I felt a lot of the work we were doing was pretty positive and helpful to the horses and riders who were coming to the clinics. On the downside, I found I was carrying around what seemed like a ton of negative baggage that wasn't doing anybody any good whatsoever and, in fact, was holding me back from moving forward in my work.

Where did all this baggage come from, I wondered, and why was it interfering so much with my overall work and, specifically, the work I was doing in the clinics? After all, doing clinics shouldn't be that hard. At the core, they are really nothing more than a job—just like any other job, when you get right down to it. Besides, I more or less knew what I was doing . . . didn't I? So why was this such a mental and physical struggle for me? Things should have been getting easier as time went on, not harder.

Then it finally dawned on me. The problem I was having had nothing to do with whether or not I was doing clinics. Clinics were ultimately just a vehicle for the work I was doing. It also had nothing to do with the things I thought were bothering me—starting with the people who came to the clinics questioning my methods and abilities. It had nothing to do with whether or not my body felt good, and it didn't even have anything to do with whether or not I was able to help the folks who came to ride in the clinics. What it really boiled down to was whether or not I was doing good work . . . work with dignity, honor, and integrity. And I had to admit, I had been falling just a little short of that. Well, maybe a *lot* short.

That was the bottom line, and I believe it was the reason I had been so bothered. Growing up working with the old man provided me with a standard, and the one word that comes to mind when I think about his work with horses is *integrity*. No matter what the situation or where he was, he always did his absolute best.

Since the time I started giving clinics, and even before to a certain extent, I realized my work had slowly stopped improving. Rather than looking for a way to get it back on track, I just started to let it slide and then began making excuses for why that was happening. And there is certainly no dignity, honor, or integrity in that.

What happened next was pretty interesting. For at least two years prior to my fall, I had been toying with the idea of getting into an aikido class to improve my balance, timing, and feel in my horse work. I knew there was a class in town at the local health club, and I even went there to sign up at one time, but the classes had been moved to another location. The day I went to the new location to sign up, the place was closed for the day and the door was locked. Then, shortly after I got home from that fateful trip to England, our family went to a fundraiser for the school our two young sons attended. Part of the fundraising was a silent auction, and one of the items was two months of aikido classes at that same dojo, the place where I had tried to sign up. I placed a substantial bid for the classes, but at the very last minute, I was outbid by someone else.

In December, I pinpointed what I felt the problem was with my work and made a mental commitment to work on eliminating some of the issues I was having. The first was to no longer allow myself to be bothered by what other people said about me or my work. From that point forward, I would be doing my absolute best, so what others said wouldn't really matter anyway . . . whether good or bad.

Two weeks after I committed to that decision, my wife Wendy and I went to a small Christmas party, one we had never been to before. One of the first people I met as we walked in the door was Shihan Eric Adams, the owner of the dojo and the aikido instructor I had been trying to hook up with for nearly two years.

The irony of the situation didn't escape me. While I was struggling with all of these issues in my work, I wasn't able to make contact with Shihan Adams. In fact, when I showed up at his dojo door, it was not only closed but also locked. Then, almost as soon as I decided I would rid myself of just one of the issues I was struggling with, Shihan Adams literally appeared right in front of me.

Was it coincidence or was it that I had finally emptied something out of my cup so that something else could fit in? Regardless, it was becoming clear I was finally back on my feet and heading down the path I had started traveling many years before. Little did I understand at the time all the new places that path was about to take me, and all the things I would learn along the way.

Top: Talking with a student in Okehampton, England.
Left: Dr. Dave Siemens, Nancy Richards, Kathleen
Lindley, and Mark, on the moors in southern England.
Right: At the clinic in Okehampton, England.

Above: Discussing equine anatomy at a week-long clinic, Loveland, Colorado.
Below: Mark and Mouse at a clinic in Hood, Oregon.

Top: Student instructor Beth Anne Doblado, Alpine, California.
Left: Mark and Beth Anne in California.
Right: Mark and his assistant, Kathleen Lindley, Alpine, California.

Right: Asking a horse to move
with focus and intent.
Below Left: The ground
crew finishing up.
Below Right: Bringing in
the pairs on branding day.
Bottom: Moving into the herd.

Top: Heading to the fire.
Bottom: Mark & Roanie
getting ready to pick up
the heels.

Left: Shihan Eric Adams at his "day job."
Right: Mark and Roanie.

Above Left:
Sensie Mark and
fellow student
Joel York.
Above Right:
Sensei Marty
Holmes.
Left: Shihan Eric
Adams, Joel York,
Sensei Marty
Holmes, & Sensei
Mark in the dojo.
Below: Shihan
Eric Adams work-
ing with Sensei
Kyya Grant.

Top: Upper-belt aikido class:
Sensei Kyya Grant (visiting from Washington and one of
Mark's student instructors), Sensei Mark, Tyler Rashid (Mark's
son), Sensei Marty Holmes, Sensei Jo Adams, Sempei Mike
Haskett, Shihan Eric Adams, and Joel York.
Left: Circular movement of aikido.
Credits: *Bringing in the Pairs, Picking up Heels, Mark Waving*—
by Dick Orleans. All others by Kathleen Lindley.

6

The New Student

I've been involved with two things pretty much my entire life. The first one is horses, the second is music. In fact, I don't think there's been a time when at least part of my means of making a living didn't involve one or the other. Sure I've had transitional jobs, such as working on a loading dock and as a truck and tractor tire "technician" (a glorified term that means I spent a lot of time changing big tires in muddy fields and scorching-hot highways). But even during those jobs, I was either playing music, working with horses, or both.

Music and horses seem to be my paths in life, so not surprisingly, most of my energies are spent crafting those activities. Almost everything I've done and continue to do revolves around them, and it has for over thirty-five years. But there I was, about to embark on a completely different journey and try something I'd never tried before . . . aikido.

While I'd been a pretty good athlete in my younger days, I'm sorry to say those days had long since passed, and my body was in shambles. Both knees had given me serious problems since my high school days. I had two herniated discs in my back, had injuries to one shoulder that required surgery, was expected to have surgery on the other shoulder before long, and had dislocated or broken so many bones over the years I'd actually lost count.

I'd moved around like I was eighty years old since my late twenties, and my physical issues were now causing me problems with my riding. Yet, there I was, in an old sweatsuit at my very first aikido class, trying to kneel in seiza, the formal position for meditation prior to beginning class. In this position the student is to kneel down and sit on his heels with the hands cupped softly in the lap, thumb and index fingers creating a small circle. The meditation time before class is designed to clear your mind and prepare you for the work ahead.

Unfortunately, the only thing on my mind right then was how much my knees were killing me. I hadn't knelt down like that in fifteen years, maybe longer, and within seconds of taking the position, I could feel my joints locking up and the muscles in my quads screaming for mercy. The meditation lasts as long as the sensei, or teacher, deems necessary, and on that first night, it seemed as though we were down for an hour, although it was really only a couple of minutes.

When the meditation is over, the command is given, and all students bow as a sign of respect to the dojo, the room in which we would practice. Then they rise in unison, ending up in *migi hanmi kamae*, the Japanese term for the basic right stance or posture. In this posture, the student stands with the knees slightly bent, right foot forward and turned to the outside. The left foot is behind the right by about twelve inches and is also turned to the outside. The right arm and hand are held about chest high and extended directly in front of the body with the fingers relaxed and slightly spread apart. The left arm and hand are held in basically the same position at belt level, so that if the fingers on both hands were closed, they would be perfectly placed to hold the handle of a sword.

At any rate, everybody had risen and was in the stance, while I was just trying to hobble up into any kind of standing position, much less the proper one. I was shocked at how difficult it was not only to get into that stance, but also to retain my balance in it. Even after my fall in England, I had still been trying to convince myself that my balance wasn't all that bad. Yet just trying to stand in a position different than what I was used to showed me that wasn't so.

If my balance wasn't nearly as good as I thought, there's no telling how much the horses I'd been riding over the last several years had been filling in for me. I don't mind telling you, the thought of how much harder they must have had to work while I was perpetually out of balance on their backs was more than just a little disheartening. My only consolation was that at least I was finally doing something about it.

As is the case with all new aikido students, I spent the rest of that first class learning how to stand in the proper right stance. When I began getting the feel of the right stance, I was then to do the same thing in the left stance, a mirror image of the right. I did this possibly 200 times on each side and was still struggling with it a little by the time class was finished. It appeared I had a long row to hoe.

There isn't a whole lot of information on the history of aikido, but it is generally believed to have had its origin in *diato ryu aikijutsu,* which is said to have been founded sometime in the mid-800s A.D. It was passed down through generations of the Minamoto family until the mid-1800s and had become primarily a samurai practice. Many of the samurai believed the true job of a warrior was to maintain peace, not cause pain, suffering, and destruction, and so the art of aikido is interesting in that it promotes peace, while at the same time being extremely dangerous and potentially deadly.

One of the mainstays of aikido is developing the ability to work *with* an attacker's energy, instead of against it. During an attack, an aikidoist will enter in, or move toward the attacker, make contact, blend with the attacker's movement, and then augment the attacker's energy and direct it to the most peaceful solution possible.

Sometimes that solution is simply moving the attacker off line and into a different direction. At times it might be something much more harmful or devastating to the attacker. Either way, the attacker's well-being is almost always taken into consideration, even while he is attacking, and that idea becomes part and parcel of how an aikidoist learns to control any attack.

Another mainstay of aikido is circular motion. There are very few moves in aikido that follow straight lines, so any time the aikidoist accepts an attack, he or she almost always initiates some kind of circular movement with the attacker, which not only takes the attacker's energy but also takes their balance.

There are really no offensive moves in aikido, which means it can only be initiated by an attacker's negative actions. Once an attack is initiated and the aikidoist and attacker have made contact, at some point both attacker and defender will be facing the same direction at the same time, thus allowing the defender to have the same physical and visual perspective the attacker had just before he attacked. This helps nurture a non-judgmental attitude in the aikidoist, which in turn helps to keep the ego in check. This is, in and of itself, another important mainstay of the art.

Seeing things from a different perspective is an extremely important concept for any horseperson. It is widely agreed that one of the biggest assets in successful training is the ability to see things from the horse's point of view. If we can do that one thing, it's a whole lot easier to accomplish goals with the horse, using the least amount of energy on everybody's part.

On one hand, my first aikido class was very discouraging because of all the trouble I had trying to perform what appeared to be something so very simple. On the other hand, it gave me new insight and an appreciation for what some of my own students must go through, whether horse or human, when I ask them to perform a task or maneuver they aren't physically or mentally familiar with.

I think teachers can lose sight of the fact that learning something new can be excruciatingly difficult for their students. I know I sure had. Going to that first aikido class and struggling like I did put me in the role of the new student, a role I hadn't been in for quite a while. I was learning all over again what it was like, and I don't mind telling you, it was no walk in the park.

On my way home from class that night, I couldn't help but think about all those people over the years who had been *my* students. I thought of all the blank stares I got when I tried to explain something they didn't comprehend and the looks of frustration they had after trying some new technique for the umpteenth time, only to have it fall short of the desired response once again.

It also made me think about the horses, and all the times they would struggle with what I was trying to show them . . . those foot stomps and head shakes, the tail swishes, and the incorrect responses that seemed to come out of nowhere. All those reactions, from both horses and humans, suddenly began to make perfect sense. It was the apprehension that appears at the beginning of any new learning process. It's the feeling of not knowing where we are, where we're going, or what we're doing. It is at this critical place that we begin to see not only how good our teacher is, but also how good we are at being students.

I went into the aikido class believing that what I learned there would ultimately help me with my horse work. Because of that belief, I went in with the attitude that, as a student, I would try anything that was asked of me, no matter what. This was a huge step for me, a big leap of faith, because within the first four or five classes, things began to get pretty physical.

We began to learn how to fall and roll, things I wasn't sure I would physically be able to do because of my back problem, and we also began to learn how to enter into an attack, instead of flee from it, and then control the attacker's energy—both things that can be intimidating if you've never done them before. Oddly enough, by just jumping in and doing what was asked of me, I found I didn't really think about my back injury all that much, and as a result, it didn't bother me nearly as much as I thought it would. In fact, within about a year's time, my back problem seemed to have all but disappeared. My knees and legs had pretty much stopped bothering me as well.

It turns out that in order to perform aikido with some semblance of accuracy, you need to use the body correctly, which was something I hadn't done in quite some time. I had allowed my back to become stiff and rigid, which in turn caused me to carry my shoulders in a position that looked as though I had shrugged them and forgot to let them back down. I walked with a perpetual slump, as if I were walking into a stiff wind.

Over time, however, my ability to perform the various moves, positions, locks, and throws improved, and so did my overall body movement. Slowly, it began to appear as though my body was actually healing itself, simply because I was being forced to use it properly once again. So, from a physical standpoint, the classes paid big dividends I hadn't thought possible just a few months earlier.

The fact that I was put in a position to see things from a student's standpoint also turned out to be a huge benefit. The way I was taught in class was different than anything I'd known in the past, and initially that presented a pretty big hurdle. For one thing, I was learning from three teachers, often at the same time, and each teacher had a slightly different way of presenting the same information. I don't mind telling you this could be more than just a little confusing.

There were times when Shihan Adams would show us a certain movement or technique, then move on to work with other students. Soon, Sensei Marty Holmes would come over, watch what we were doing, and then ask us to make certain adjustments. These adjustments were sometimes different than what Shihan Adams had showed us, but we would make the adjustments and continue our work.

A little while later Sensei Jo Adams, Shihan Adams' mother, would come along and also ask us to make adjustments to what we were doing. Again, these adjustments were sometimes different from what Shihan Adams and Sensei Marty had told us to do, but we would make the adjustments anyway and continue on. Eventually Shihan Adams would come back around, watch what we were doing, and often make adjustments, so we were back to doing what he had originally shown us.

Early on, this way of being taught got pretty frustrating, and in fact there were quite a few times in the beginning when either myself or another student started the "yeah, buts." One instructor would ask us to perform a technique a certain way, and then another teacher came around and asked us to perform it differently. As the second instructor finished his explanation, one of us might say, "Yeah, but Sensei Marty just said we should do it this way."

The instructor would listen patiently to our often-feeble attempt to explain a technique he had performed perhaps a thousand times.

When we had finished, he usually nodded, smiled, and asked us to go ahead and try it his way anyway, which we always did.

What we didn't realize at the time was that pretty much everything we did or learned in class would ultimately become an extension of the *way* of aikido. Even this approach to how we were being taught was an exercise in aikido. At its core, aikido is all about blending and going with whatever is being presented. So when different ways of performing the same technique are presented by different teachers, the idea wasn't to look at it as a problem, it was to find a way to go with it and then use it to your advantage.

Over time I realized that hearing the same information in different ways was a good thing. After all, when it comes to aikido, the principles of the techniques and methods are pretty much always going to be the same. But the variations of those techniques and methods are endless. Understanding as many perspectives as possible keeps that many more options available to us when we're presented with real-life situations. It didn't take long before I began to see a number of correlations between this way of thinking and horsemanship. In both, the more variations we can learn of any one technique or method or idea, the better off we will ultimately be.

In horsemanship, as in aikido, the principles behind the techniques and methods are generally going to be the same, no matter who is teaching them—provided, of course, that the teacher has a strong understanding of the principles. Problems arise when the teacher misunderstands the principles. Then a skewed version of a technique or method ends up being taught and ultimately passed on to future generations of students.

I'm beginning to see that the people who are truly good at their chosen craft, art, or profession are the ones who can make things look effortless, whether they are performing the task themselves or teaching it to others. They may give the impression they have been performing the craft all their lives, and in fact they often look as though they were born doing it. Yet, what we don't see and sometimes fail to appreciate is the countless hours they have spent practicing their chosen craft. It is that practice and dedication that has gotten them where they are, as well as the time and dedication of *their* teachers.

I recall working with the old man back when I was a kid and he was one of those who possessed that effortlessness in his work. He made working with horses look so easy that even when he worked with the most rank of the rank, I never saw him get rattled. He always appeared in total control of the situation. He was really pretty amazing to watch, because he could easily switch from one idea to the next during the most difficult of situations without the slightest hesitation. As a teacher, he did the same thing with me.

I would have to say his teaching method, whether with horses or people, reflected the way he lived his life . . . quiet and easy going. It was obviously important to him that I understood what he was trying to pass along, but it was never so important that he felt the need to make me feel bad, belittle me, or give up if I didn't get it right away. If I didn't understand a concept he was trying to impart, he simply switched gears and presented it in a different way or sometimes just asked me to try again. And in my opinion, this is not only the sign of a truly gifted horseman, it's the sign of a truly gifted teacher.

I have to admit, I didn't really think I would ever run into anyone else like him, and in fact, until I began studying aikido, I hadn't. However, it wasn't long after I started my training that I began to see eerie similarities between the old man's way of teaching and the way Shihan Adams taught. There were a couple of incidents, in particular, that brought this home to me.

The first happened years ago when I was working with a fairly new horse named Ring that had arrived at the old man's place a week or so before. He was a young quarter horse gelding that had apparently been named for an unusual, oblong, white ring on his left flank. Overall he was a pretty nice fellow with only one apparent problem. Anytime one of us rode him to the far end of the arena, he'd suddenly bolt back toward the barn at the other end. I had ridden him a number of times during the week that we'd had him, and he'd done the same thing each time. By the second time I rode him, I'd already found that once he decided to go, there just didn't seem to be anything I could do to stop him.

The old man came out and watched as Ring and I charged uncontrollably back from the far end of the arena for the fifth or sixth time in less than ten minutes. With his ever-present cigarette between his fingers, he called me over to where he was leaning on the fence.

"He starts to think about bolting right over there." He pointed his nicotine-stained fingers toward a spot near the far end. "That's when you've got to get him thinking about something else. If you go past that spot without doing anything, he's gonna be gone."

"I know," I agreed, "but he's too quick for me."

"He won't be, if you get him just before that spot, there." He pointed again.

"What should I do, though?" The question was more of a plea for help than an actual query.

"Just before that spot," he said, as he flicked the ash from his cigarette, "take your inside rein and bring his head around into a tight turn. He'll want to run when you do that, so just be patient. Let him move in the circle until he relaxes a bit and then let him go straight again."

"But what if he tries to bolt when I let him go straight?"

"Then put him back in the circle 'til he relaxes again." He took a drag from his cigarette. "Go on now, give it a try."

We rode down toward the other end of the arena, and just as we got close to where I thought the old man had pointed, Ring bolted. I tried to turn him with my inside rein, but I was way too late.

We got back to the other end of the arena in record time, and after I got Ring smoothed out a little, I rode back over to the old man.

"I tried to turn him right there where you said," I blurted, before he could even get a word out, "but he's just too quick for me."

"Well," he nodded, "go give it another try."

I let out an exasperated sigh, turned Ring back toward the far end, and rode off. Again, just as we got about to where the old man wanted me to circle him, Ring bolted. I rode back up to where the old man was standing near the fence.

"When we got to that spot," I explained, "I took ahold of the rein like this and pulled, but he just stuck his nose out and pulled the other way. I kept trying to get his head around, but the next thing I knew we were back down here."

The old man just nodded, and asked me to try again. This went on for the next half-hour, with Ring and I riding down to the far end of the arena and then flying back. Each time Ring bolted, I rode up to the old man and explained why his plan didn't work. Each time he listened patiently to what I had to say and asked me to try again.

Eventually, after Lord knows how many trips out and back, I finally ran out of excuses for why his plan wasn't working, and I didn't stop to talk to the old man after we'd bolted back. Instead, I just rode past him back toward the far end.

This time, however, something was different. About ten feet before we reached the spot where Ring usually bolted, I felt him begin to tense up, and I took the inside rein and turned him. He circled a few times, and I felt his body soften a little. I let him go straight for a few steps, until he started to tighten again. I turned him, and again he softened.

We did this a number of times, and because I was concentrating so hard on feeling what Ring was doing, I hadn't been paying any attention to where we were in the arena. Finally Ring got soft and stayed soft, and it was then that I looked up for the first time. Lo and behold, we had made it all the way around the arena without bolting. I brought Ring to a stop about twenty feet from where the old man was standing.

"There," he nodded, with a little smile. "Now *that's* how you do that."

The second incident happened about two-and-a-half years after my first aikido class. I had advanced through the ranks and, now as a green belt, was working on more advanced moves. During this class, we were working on a throw known as *iriminage* for the first time. In *iriminage,* the attacker is striking from the front with an overhead blow to the head. We were to enter into the attack, blend with the blow, and then direct it slightly downward, as we spun a small circle to the right, slightly away from the attacker, on a pivot foot. Just before the attacker falls from being directed downward, the pivot is reversed, and we were to move into the attacker, throwing him on his back.

We had been working on the move for perhaps fifteen minutes when Shihan Adams came over. It was obvious we were all struggling, so he stepped in to demonstrate how the move should look and work. We watched carefully, and when he was finished, he asked me to give it a try.

My partner initiated the attack, and I moved in an attempt to blend with it. Then I tried to pivot, but that was obviously where I was having trouble. Almost immediately the move fell apart. When I tried to pivot, my back and hips weren't moving the way they should, and as a result my right leg wouldn't swing back around to the right, behind me, like it should.

"I guess I'm having trouble getting my right foot back," I explained to Shihan.

"Let's try it again," he smiled.

For the next several minutes, I tried the move over and over, and each time I missed it. Invariably, I turned to Shihan and explained to him why I was missing the move, and each time he smiled, nodded, and asked me to try again. Before long—just like that day with the old man and Ring—I just sort of ran out of excuses, so I quit offering any. Only then did the move finally come through.

My partner attacked, I blended with him, directed him downward and pivoted slightly away. Just before he fell forward, I reversed the pivot, which nearly lifted him off his feet as he fell backward. The entire move felt soft and effortless, which surprised me. With my partner lying on the mat, I turned and looked at my teacher.

"There," Shihan nodded, with a smile. "Now *that's* how you do that!"

As you can see, the similarities between these two situations are more than just a little bit spooky. In both cases I was working with a partner, one being a horse, the other a human, and the key to success in both tasks hinged on whether or not I could execute some type of circular movement. With Ring it was a turn using his entire body; with my aikido partner it was performing a pivot with my own body.

In both cases I allowed my own mental baggage to get in the way of performing the circles, which in turn prevented me from accomplishing the tasks. In both cases I spent a great deal of time telling my teachers all the reasons why I couldn't accomplish the tasks, not realizing that both were well aware of what was going on. After all, both men had already traveled down the road I was on and probably had gone through what I was going through hundreds of times before.

Yet both men still allowed me to say what I felt I needed to say, while keeping me focused on the task at hand. Eventually, having been allowed to exhaust all my excuses, there was apparently nothing left for me to do but get the task done correctly, which I was finally able to do.

In these two cases, the teachers allowed what needed to happen, happen. They entered in (by showing up at just the right time), went *with* what was being presented to them, and directed the situation to the most peaceful solution possible—without being judgmental or allowing their own ego to get involved. To me, this is, in microcosm, what aikido is all about and what horsemanship is all about. It is the way of harmony.

Early on I had been taught to always try to work *with* horses, not against them, to always strive for harmony in my work with them. This was the path I thought I was on with my horsemanship, and I suppose to some extent it *was* the path I was on. What I was now learning, however, was there was a whole lot more to understand about being in harmony—whether with a horse, another human, one's self, or with the world around me.

It was my good fortune that the path I'd been on had led me where I was. It was a pretty nice place to be and one I had been comfortable in for quite a while. However, it became very clear the time had come to make a change. It was a change that would come slowly and one I am still working on to this day. But before that change could even begin to happen, I had to reach an understanding about how the principles of aikido—the way of harmony—would play out in the world of horsemanship I already knew.

7

The Art of "Going With"

Most animals would be great at martial arts. In particular, they would be great aikidoists. Like horsemanship, when aikido is performed properly, it is done without malice, without muscle, without ego, and without intent to do harm. Which brings us back to animals being good aikidoists.

We have five dogs at our house, all border collies or a border-collie mix. As anyone who has been around border collies can attest, they are a breed with boundless energy. Two of our dogs are young and spend a great deal of time playing with one another. Buster, the bigger of the two, runs across the yard and jumps at Riley, his brother. Just before Buster makes contact, Riley moves and rolls with Buster's energy.

Next thing you know, Riley is on top of Buster. Then Buster moves with Riley's energy, and suddenly he's on top. The entire time both dogs keep moving, circling, dipping, leaping, rolling, and most of all, having fun, but they almost always do it by using each other's energy. You see the same behavior when cats and other animals, wild or domestic, play.

If you watch horses play, run out in the pasture, or even fight, you almost always get a chance to see aikido techniques at work. When they're playing, one horse jumps on or bumps into another, and the other horse usually rolls with the movement, instead of pushing back against it. As several horses run across the pasture together, one turns, and they all turn in unison. If you watch one horse move another from the feed, very often all it takes is an ear flick or slight head toss to initiate movement.

Horses, like other animals, don't always roll with the energy of an opponent, but given the opportunity to go with that energy, instead of fighting it, a horse almost always opts for "going with." This trait is, in my opinion, one of the reasons why humans like horses so much.

This "going with" may appear to us as if the horse is allowing itself to be dominated. We like things we can dominate. Makes us feel superior, I guess. Yet, when we take a good hard look at our relationships with horses, we have to ask ourselves this question. Is the horse truly allowing itself to be dominated or has it simply found a way to "go with" us as a means of survival?

Humans are real good at getting rid of things we feel are of no use; this includes animals and even other humans, for that matter. Yet the domestic horse is thriving right now, due to the fact that we see a benefit in keeping them around, mostly as pets or tools or showpieces. Wild horses, on the other hand, are in a different situation.

For quite a while, there's been a movement to eliminate wild horses from the BLM public lands where they roam. Why? Well, some folks see the wild horse as having no purpose. In fact, to some, they're just a major expense—they compete with cattle for grass and water. So, many people just want them gone.

Our tendency to rid ourselves of things we don't need could take unexpected turns, including one that would affect the same people who want the wild horses eliminated. What would happen if everybody stopped eating beef? We would no longer have any use for beef cattle, and it's very possible that cattle could become extinct. What other use would we have for cattle?

For any animal, certainly one as large and as high-maintenance as the horse, to survive in our world, it must first be of some benefit to us. The horse has certainly proven himself to be just that. As a result, we can see our way clear to keeping him around. That again begs the question—are horses truly that easily dominated by humans, making them desirable to us, or have they simply found a way to "go with" us so they can survive?

The ability to "go with" situations is a key element in aikido, but it's not always easy to learn. Humans, you see, are notoriously bad about being able to "go with" when it involves a change in their normal way of doing things. It's in our nature to fight change. That's why, even though I was facing all kinds of problems in my horse work, I still resisted doing anything about it. Put simply, I had fallen into certain patterns I was comfortable with, both mentally and physically. They weren't particularly positive patterns—in fact, they were pretty detrimental overall—but yet I still couldn't see my way out, even when opportunities for change presented themselves.

There's no question in my mind that there is an art to being able to simply "go with." You can, for instance, take the idea too far. If you "go with" to the point of being uncommitted to your beliefs, you end up being tossed around like a leaf in the wind. On the other hand, if you try to "go with" but are too committed to your beliefs, you will create a brace within yourself that ultimately stops the flow of information, movement, or energy that is trying to come in.

Personally, I thought I had a pretty good handle on what it meant to be able to "go with," whether in my horsemanship or in my everyday life. Then I began training in aikido and saw how much I had to learn about the subject. It wasn't long before I realized that there were many, many layers to the concept and that I was barely scratching the surface. A case in point was something I noticed about a year into my training; I couldn't help but draw parallels between it and what I see so often in the horse world.

The very first thing I learned when I began my aikido training was the proper etiquette for bowing in, prior to the beginning of class. In particular, I was shown where in the dojo I was to stand in relationship to the higher-ranking students. All students stand in a line facing the instructor at the front of the dojo. The lower the rank you have, the farther to the left you stand. For the first several months of my training, I was relegated to standing as far to the left as possible. In fact, the only thing farther to the left was the wall.

The rank each student holds is not only designated by where they stand in line, but also by the color of his or her belt. The first level's belt color is white. Now, the only thing you have to do to get a white belt is show up for the first class. In fact, if you did nothing more than go out and buy a *gi*, the traditional martial art "uniform," you'd have a white belt, because that's what it comes with.

A white belt signifies you have very little, if any, knowledge of the art you are pursuing. It tells everyone in class you are a new student and at the very beginning of your journey. At this point, you probably will not be interested in sparring with the black belts, who are clear down on the right. For a white belt, the right side of the dojo line seems like a very long way away, both physically and mentally.

Early on, having abandoned my sweat suit, I stood on the left side of the dojo in my brand-new, stiff, almost shiny white *gi*, with creases still in the sleeves and legs from the original package, and I recall looking in awe at those black belts. Their *gis* were an off-white or yellow-white, with sweat- and dirt-stained collars, knees, elbows, and armpits. There were even small bloodstains here and there. Bloodstains, for crying out loud! A daunting thought for someone just starting out.

As you gain more knowledge and understanding, you're promoted to the next level, the yellow belt. You can now work with other yellow belts, with white belts, or sometimes with orange belts, just a level above you. But you still aren't going to work with the black belts.

Before long you may become an orange belt. Now you are allowed to work with the white and yellow belts, as well as with other orange belts. Sometimes you will work with the blue belts, the level just above you, but you're still going to stay away from the black belts.

After more time passes, you may be promoted to a blue belt. Now you can work with all the levels below you, as well as with other blue belts and the occasional purple belt above you. You're still staying away from the right side, where those black belts are throwing each other all over the place and doing things with their bodies you can only dream of.

With hard work and dedication, you are promoted to the next level, which is purple. Now you are no longer working much with the lower-level belts. Instead you are spending time with blue, purple, and green belts, the next level. Something else happens once you reach the purple level. Suddenly you're expected to start "growing up" within the dojo. You're no longer a beginner and are no longer treated as one. Your teachers' expectations clearly are higher. Prior to getting your purple belt, your mistakes were readily forgiven, but at this level a mistake may mean that you or your partner gets hurt. Nobody wants that.

Your responsibilities as a martial artist are starting to become apparent. The higher your rank, the more you are expected to do no harm . . . to yourself, your partner, and anybody around you. Those responsibilities continue to increase as you move through the ranks from purple to green, then to brown, with its three levels, and finally to black, where there are ten degrees.

To folks outside the world of martial arts, the term "black belt" conjures up the idea of a dangerous person, one not to be trifled with. In one sense that's true. However, to most martial artists, reaching the black-belt level simply means their peers and teachers now consider them a serious student of their chosen art.

I bring up the concept of levels of knowledge in aikido because, as I mentioned, there are very strong parallels between those levels of knowledge, the art of "going with," and horsemanship. Finding those parallels gave me a different perspective on my work and a new level of understanding of the folks I worked with.

Ann brought the horse to the clinic because she was feeling pretty overwhelmed. She'd owned the horse since he was a long yearling and planned to make him into a quiet trail horse for herself and her daughter. Ann was fairly new to horses at the time, having only been around them for four years or so, and this particular horse had been the first she owned.

She'd always loved horses and always wanted one, but by her own admission, she had almost no experience with them when she got her horse. At the age of thirty-six, with a little disposable income and some property in the country large enough for a couple of horses, she decided she'd finally act upon her dream. Up to that point, she had only ridden dude horses on trail rides while on vacation, and she knew that with her limited knowledge, she would need some help. So she began by taking lessons at a local riding stable.

Within six months Ann was not only taking lessons at the barn, she was helping out around the place, mucking out stalls, feeding, and cleaning water tanks. After about a year, her instructor told her she should start thinking about buying a horse, and the instructor knew just the one for her. It was the yearling the instructor was raising. The yearling was out of his mare, an Arabian/quarter horse cross, and he told Ann the little gelding would be perfect for her. Ann was concerned about her lack of knowledge and the gelding's young age, but he assured her they would form a great partnership and learn together. He also told Ann he would help them every step of the way.

Ann spent time with the colt for several weeks, and the two seemed to get along real well. It wasn't long before she had fallen in love with the little guy. So, just over a year from the time she'd taken her first riding lesson, she bought her first horse, the yearling gelding she named Sandy. She called him that because he had a strong propensity for rolling in the sand every chance he got.

Things went along very well for the two of them for the next year-and-a-half, when a number of folks at the barn, including her instructor, started telling her it was time to get Sandy started under saddle. Her instructor suggested Ann take him to a colt-starting clinic nearby, but she had serious reservations about starting Sandy in a clinic because she didn't feel he was mentally ready. She also didn't think she had enough skill to do the work properly. Her instructor assured her everything would be fine, so after much deliberation, off she went.

By all accounts, both Sandy and Ann struggled at the clinic. Ann felt that much of the information presented was way over her head. At one point, perhaps out of frustration, the trainer conducting the clinic suggested that maybe Ann wasn't really cut out for working with horses. Ann later told me she felt the trainer was not only correct in saying that, but that she had felt the same way even before she went to the clinic.

What happened in Ann's case was that she had given up her beliefs that she and her horse weren't ready in an attempt at "going with" those she thought knew better than she did. As a result, she ended up in a situation that wasn't very beneficial to either her or her horse. In fact, she ended up losing ground in her horsemanship, because her confidence had been shaken. Had she chosen to "go with" her own instincts and beliefs, which in this case were correct, the entire problem could have been avoided.

Looking at Ann's situation from another perspective, if Ann had been a martial artist instead of a horse person, her skill level would have perhaps been equivalent to that of an orange belt. Yet, everyone around her, including her instructor and the trainer she took her colt to, were pushing her to try to perform black-belt maneuvers. In a dojo, that would have been totally unacceptable, due to the possible harm it could have caused. Yet when it comes to horses and horse people, this type of thing happens all the time and hardly anybody gives it a second thought.

Chuck's horse was constantly bumping into him. It didn't matter if Chuck was leading him from one place to another or if the two were just standing side by side. When the two stood next to each other, the horse constantly nudged him with his head, often knocking Chuck off balance. We were only about five minutes into Chuck's session on the first day of the clinic when an auditor raised her hand.

"Are you going to do something about that horse's disrespectful behavior?" she asked.

"What disrespectful behavior is that?" I questioned.

"He's all over Chuck," she said, pointing at the horse as he bumped Chuck with his head.

"Is this something you've ever worked on with this horse?" I asked, turning to Chuck.

"What? Him rubbing his head on me like this?" Chuck answered.

"Yes," I nodded. "Have you ever asked him not to do that?"

"No," he replied. "I don't mind it."

"But you're teaching him to be disrespectful," the woman said, in an almost shocked voice.

"I don't really see it as being disrespectful," Chuck answered.

"You see it as disrespect," she aimed her question at me, "don't you?"

"Not really," I said with a shrug. "In fact, I see it as just the opposite. Here, Chuck is allowing his horse to rub on him, so basically he's teaching the horse it's okay to do it. In turn, the horse is doing what Chuck is teaching, so in a sense, the horse is actually being very obedient."

"Every other trainer I've ever seen would say that horse is disrespecting Chuck's space," the woman argued.

I went on to explain that I thought the horse's behavior could only be disrespectful if Chuck didn't want him to do it, which wasn't the case, and if Chuck had already explained to the horse the behavior was unacceptable, which he hadn't done.

"I guess maybe it's just a little different way of looking at it," I remarked. "I just feel, in cases like this, if we call the horse's behavior disrespectful, then basically what we're doing is placing the blame for the behavior on the horse. In reality the only reason he's doing it in the first place is because a human has taught it to him."

"I guess I would have to disagree," the woman said with a smile. And with that, the discussion was over.

So here's a different example of a person trying to "go with." In the auditor's case, she'd been gathering information about working with horses from a number of trainers. She'd found a style of horsemanship that resonated with her, so she was seeing as many trainers as she could who she thought shared that style.

Most of those trainers had much the same view of a horse being "disrespectful," and so, over time, that view became her view. She was so committed to that viewpoint that she wasn't able to break away from it. She was closing the door on the possibility there could be another reason, other than the one she believed to be true, for the horse's behavior. It appeared as though she had set up an internal brace that effectively prevented a flow of information or ideas from going in.

I'm not saying that my view on the subject of disrespect is absolutely correct either. However, for me, a key to the art of "going with" is keeping as many options available as possible. It seems to me that only when we are able to keep our options open are we able to make the most appropriate decision at the most appropriate time.

Sara came to one of the clinics wanting to work on flying lead changes and sliding stops with her horse. On the first day, I asked her how much experience she had with horses, and she told me without hesitation that she had twenty-two years of experience.

As we began working with Sara and her horse, it became clear that she was indeed a very good rider. She had a great seat and her balance was nearly impeccable. However, she seemed to lack a few basic training skills, most importantly the timing and placement of her cues, along with the amount of pressure she used to apply cues. Getting her horse to do flying lead changes and sliding stops was pretty much out of the question, only because of the confusion she was inadvertently causing in her horse. So for three days we worked exclusively on improving her feel, timing, and awareness in the saddle, and on the last day we began working on her lead changes.

She probably worked harder than anybody else in that particular clinic, and because of her dedication to the work she was doing, we were able to get a couple of nice lead changes by the time she was finished.

"You remember the first day when you asked me how much horse experience I had?" she asked, after the clinic was over.

"Yes," I nodded.

"I told you I had twenty-two years of experience," she smiled, "but that wasn't quite the truth."

"How's that?"

"Well, after these last four days, what I've come to understand," she was still smiling, "is I've actually only had one year of experience . . . twenty-two times."

She went on to say that after all those years of working with horses, she was feeling like the kid who couldn't read in school but got promoted to the next grade anyway. She could see where, years ago, she had gotten a few of the basics down and then jumped right up to the next thing, then the next, and the next. Yet she hadn't really, *truly* understood any of what she was doing. She could see not only why she was having so much trouble getting her horse to do lead changes and stops, but also why she was having trouble in a number of other areas as well.

I believe what she was saying was that she had been in such a hurry to become an accomplished horsewoman (a black belt) that she skipped a number of important steps that would have helped get her there. As a result, she was constantly falling short of her goal. What this boiled down to was that she never allowed herself to become happy with where she was in her horsemanship, regardless of her level.

Each step we go through in our learning process—whether it's in horsemanship, martial arts, mathematics, sports, computers, or whatever—is there for a reason. If we skip or just breeze over any step or any part of a step, we're missing critical information, information that will benefit us at the next level. Skipping steps is pretty rampant in the horse world. An inexperienced person goes to this clinic or that clinic or watches his favorite trainer perform a certain, very spectacular maneuver, and right away that person wants to be able to perform just like that.

Unfortunately, it just doesn't work that way. In fact, the average person can become a master in very few activities in life without first putting in years of hard work. With limited experience at the game of golf, for instance, you wouldn't expect to buy a set of golf clubs, go out the next day, and be able to play par golf. But that's basically what we see a lot of horse people try to do.

For me, one of the best parts of working with horses is learning how to go through the steps. It's what gives me the understanding I need to do the work well. I feel that a big part of being able to learn the steps starts with being truly happy with where you are in your own learning or level of expertise. In other words, it's about learning how to "go with" your personal learning process and knowing that process will be different for each person.

Now, when I say you should try to be happy with where you are in your learning, that doesn't mean you need to be satisfied. Being happy just means you accept (or "go with") where you're at any particular time. Once you learn how to accept where you are, you're able to take in as much of that level as it has to offer. And *that* is what will ultimately move you to the next level. If you don't accept where you are in your learning, you will constantly be looking past where you are and ultimately miss most of what you need to learn while you're there.

In the dojo, the student with the yellow belt is almost always working out at the same time and in the same place as the student with the black belt. So, from very early on in his training, the yellow-belt student is exposed to black-belt information. He will be able to watch those black belts working on their throws, falls, and joint locks at speeds that may seem unattainable. Yet, the yellow belt, while he may be envious of the work being done by those high-ranking students, is not allowed to try those techniques, because he simply isn't prepared to perform them safely.

One day, all that will change, and that yellow-belt student will graduate and be able to study with those upper-level belts. Not yet, though. As a yellow belt, that student will be asked to be happy at his current level of skill and knowledge. Be happy with it, yes. Accept it, yes. But not be satisfied with it.

He may not even realize it at the time, but by accepting where he is in his level of knowledge and skill, the student is beginning to learn the art of "going with."

8

Chain of Knowledge

Looking at the colt through the late afternoon haze, it was hard to believe this was the first time he'd ever carried a rider on his back. The old man had been on him for about an hour, and the red dun gelding was already going around as though he'd been ridden all his life.

The old man had me work with the colt quite a bit over the previous days, mostly on longeing and ground driving. The idea behind ground driving was to teach the little guy how to stop, back, and turn without having someone on his back. It was the old man's theory that one of the main reasons a colt goes to bucking and pitching fits the first time someone gets on its back is that the colt has very limited knowledge about what is happening and gets overwhelmed with unfamiliar information. Once a colt is overwhelmed, it has a tendency to panic and start trying to defend itself by bucking, running away, or any number of other self-protection mechanisms.

For a young horse being started for the first time, the amount of information it is being asked to absorb, both physically and mentally, is pretty daunting. First, the colt is taken away from the only job it's ever known, which is simply being a young horse out in the pasture with other young horses. Then, a saddle pad or blanket and an often ill-fitting saddle are strapped to its back.

This heavy, rigid, funny smelling piece of leather often restricts the horse's natural movement in a number of areas—something that can be extremely worrisome to an animal used to a body that moves freely. Then a leather headstall is strapped to its head and a metal bit is put in its mouth, sometimes with care, sometimes without. While the colt is trying to push this foreign, metal object out of its mouth with its tongue, a rider climbs up into the saddle on its back. The colt is then expected to carry the rider's weight and be directed by that bit, neither of which it understands to begin with.

The old man's idea of starting a colt was a little different. He had several very deliberate steps he went through with a young horse, each one designed to build on the last and each one helping create a chain of knowledge, all to give the horse an understanding of what it was going through.

It started with the simple, incidental handling of the colt—trimming feet, catching, leading, vet work, grooming, trailer loading, and the like. Along with the obvious reasons for doing these things, they were designed to get the colt used to the idea that things were going to be happening to it, more things than just being left alone in the pasture with its buddies.

From there, the old man taught the young horse how to longe, and he did so in a very specific way. He put the horse on a long cotton rope, usually about thirty feet long, attached to the halter. He would then ask the horse to circle around him at a walk and trot. As the horse moved, the old man would move with him, positioning himself about ten feet or so off the colt's inside hip, the one closest to the middle of the pen where the old man was walking.

If he wanted the colt to walk, the old man would walk relatively slowly on the inside of the circle. If he wanted the colt to trot, the old man would move into a more brisk walk. Often when he worked a horse on a longe in this way, it appeared as though the two of them were dancing together, because his cues to the horse were so subtle, you might have trouble seeing them if you didn't know what to look for.

At the time, I didn't think too much about the way the old man started his colts. As far as I knew, that was just the way it was done. Longeing was what you did before you did anything else. Of course, now I can see there were several reasons why he chose to longe young horses this way. The first, I believe, has to do with the way young horses see the world around them and, in turn, how they learn from it.

In a herd situation, from the time baby horses are born until they are about a year old (or until the mothers wean them), they can pretty much do and go anywhere they want within the herd. For the most part, they can eat when and where they want, drink when and where they want, and run into, over, or under nearly any other horse in the herd with impunity. In general they just go around and learn how to be a baby horse. The herd gives the babies a chance to learn how to make some decisions for themselves at an early age.

However, once the mothers wean them or they get to be about a year old, that all changes almost overnight, and the herd starts treating them differently. Each horse they come in contact with begins to put them in their proper place within the herd hierarchy. Suddenly the babies are told when to eat and where, they must wait their turn to drink, and running into, over, or under other horses is no longer tolerated. The babies are beginning to learn how to grow up and become productive members of the herd. And they're being taught how to turn some of their decision-making over to others.

In many domestic horse situations, young horses don't get the chance to grow up in a true herd, and so they don't have the opportunity to learn how to become grown-up horses the way they were meant to. As a result, when we begin to work with them (getting them started under saddle, for instance), many still have the mentality of a baby horse. That is, they often feel they should be able to make their own decisions, go anywhere they want, and do anything they want, any time they want.

It is my belief that a big part of starting a young horse entails helping it grow from being a baby to being an adult by teaching it how to turn over some of the decision-making to us. Personally, I feel it's better if this is done *before* we actually get on its back, and the way the old man used the longe line with his young horses is the first step in this process. It's a way to teach the colt how to do something that is out of the realm of a horse just being a horse, yet it's relatively easy for the horse to perform and gets it thinking about turning over some decisions to the person on the other end of the rope.

The second and probably more important benefit to longeing is that it prepares the horse for the next step in the process, ground driving. In ground driving, a second long cotton rope is attached to the other side of the halter. The colt is asked to longe, which by that time is something it already knows. As it is longeing, we slowly begin to guide it into turns, stops, and backing, using the two lines attached to the halter.

Teaching the colt how to stop, turn, and back during ground driving helps limit its confusion about doing those things once we climb on its back for the first time. That way, all the horse really has to worry about is the awkwardness of carrying the weight of a rider.

The old man broke down the initial saddling process in a similar fashion. He started by rubbing soft cotton ropes all over the colt (something that the longeing and ground driving also helped). Then he took one of the ropes and slid it up over the colt's back and down around its belly in the area where a cinch would go. By applying pressure with the rope in that area, he simulated the pressure of a cinch. Once the colt was okay with that pressure, the old man placed a very small, light saddle on its back and went through the longeing and ground driving process again. Over time, he increased the size and weight of the saddle until the colt was wearing the saddle that would be used in riding it.

From there, it was just a matter of time before the colt was ready to accept the weight of a rider. Looking back, it's pretty easy to see how each step the old man used in starting a colt led to the next step. Catching led to leading; leading led to longeing; longeing led to ground driving; ground driving led to stopping, turning, and backing when someone was on the horse's back.

Each time the old man went through one of these steps with a colt, he was doing what I now refer to as adding a link to the colt's chain of knowledge. I use that term because I feel it's the best way to describe the process we all go through, whether horse or human, when we're learning something new.

For instance, the great authors of the world didn't start out being able to write magnificent pieces of literature. Before they could even think about writing a book, a line of poetry, or a simple phrase, for that matter, they first had to learn the alphabet. That was the first link in their "writing" chain. They learned the sound of each letter and its place in the alphabet, what it took to write the letter on a piece of paper, and how to put the letters together to form words. Once they learned how to form words, the next link was putting them in a certain order to form cohesive sentences.

Years of practice then took place, forming the fifth link, as they wrote hundreds of letters, did schoolwork, and wrote in diaries and journals. All the time they were learning new and more sophisticated words and sentence structures and how to join them into coherent thoughts that could be read and understood by generations of people to come.

Still, it all starts with forming that very first link in the chain. Without that link, it can be argued that none of the others would have followed. To me, it is extremely important to understand the concept of links of knowledge fitting together in the proper order, no matter what endeavor we're trying to learn.

We humans often seem to look for the quickest way to learn a new skill, not necessarily the best way. As a result, we sometimes have a tendency to skip many of the essential steps that help ensure mastery of the skill. By skipping steps, we run the risk of having weak or missing links in our chain. By not having a relatively complete understanding of the thing we're trying to learn, our chain of knowledge on the skill will only go so far. Then it will stop.

Over the years, I've noticed we tend to slip into an interesting frame of mind nearly every time we're presented with a situation where we've reached the end of our chain of knowledge. For most folks, the first thing that happens is that they become frustrated, sometimes very frustrated. This is something we have in common with horses, because any time they reach the end of their chain of knowledge, they, too, get pretty frustrated.

However, the similarity seems to end there. Once the frustration and worry of the unknown has set in, there are some very distinct differences between how horses and humans handle things. A horse's response is usually pretty straightforward. When they're no longer able to comprehend a certain task or situation, horses switch over to the one thing that has kept their species alive all these years . . . instinct. Generally, this means a horse will try to flee the situation (either physically or mentally) or defend itself from it, if fleeing isn't an option.

The younger the horse, the more likely it is that instinct will take over. Older horses have more life experiences and, therefore, more of a knowledge chain to draw upon to help figure out a situation. For instance, consider the first time a saddle is strapped onto a colt. If the colt has had little or no preparation in how to accept and carry it, the chances of the colt trying to buck the saddle off his back are pretty good. Or he may panic and try to run out from underneath it. He may even do both. Yet, when the time is taken to explain the saddling process to the colt in a way that makes sense, he will generally simply accept the saddle as just another step in the process, another link in the chain, and probably won't feel the need to buck or run off.

Now, when the frustration and worry of the unknown affects humans, we may have a number of different reactions. We might react with anger and try to force a solution to the issue. Another way we might react is with unchanged repetition, making the same unsuccessful efforts over and over and expecting a different result. We may also react with resignation and abandon our efforts completely.

Still another way to respond is with deliberation. Seeing that we are in over our heads, we may step back from the situation and start looking for ways to gain enough knowledge to come up with a workable solution.

Now, while we have all these options when we come across a problem where we're a little lost, it's the last option that gives us the best opportunity for growth. Unfortunately, it is usually the most difficult one for us to choose, because our egos tend to get in the way of common sense. After all, it can be pretty hard to admit when we've come up against a situation we thought we were prepared for, but really weren't. It's not an easy thing, coming to the last link in our chain of knowledge.

❧

Looking back, maybe even as far back as when I was watching the old man ride that colt all those years ago, I believe I probably had a passing understanding of how this idea of the chain of knowledge worked. In fact, up until my fall in England, I might have thought my particular chain was relatively lengthy. The truth is that while I may have had a number of links for my chain back then, I'm not entirely sure they were all attached. In fact, I can now see there were some links I thought I had but actually didn't and others I had that I didn't even know I had!

As I looked outside the world of horses and into the world of martial arts for some help with my work, the flaws in my chain of knowledge slowly began to show themselves. At first this was discouraging, having worked pretty hard at my craft over the years and having reached a small level of success in my field. As these incongruities appeared and I began to work on them, it often felt as though I was taking steps backward in my learning, instead of forward. So much so, in fact, that for about nine months after starting aikido, I felt as though I were wandering around in some kind of fog in terms of what I knew and what I didn't know—in both aikido and my horsemanship.

As time went on, five basic principles began to emerge through my training in aikido. It was these five principles—awareness, commitment, staying centered, understanding and performing circular movement, and honoring our teachers and our places of learning—that not only helped me lengthen and strengthen my chain of knowledge, but also put me back on the track with horses I had started down so many years before.

As I developed a feel for these five principles, I was amazed at how easily they could be applied positively to my work with horses and, in turn, how much they could positively affect the rest of my life, as well.

9

Awareness

It was part of my morning routine. I took three scoops of oats out of the big bin and placed one in each of the feed boxes in the first three tie stalls. Then I went to the back door of the barn and opened the top of the big Dutch door to see the three old horses patiently waiting there for their breakfast.

These three horses were the geriatric members of the old man's herd, two geldings and one mare, and for the most part their days were spent just grazing in the back pasture. Every morning, however, they made their way up to the barn and stood by the back door. I swung the bottom half of the Dutch door open, and they quietly filed in. First the gelding named Bullet, then the mare, Abby, and finally the other old gelding, Sox.

They entered in single file and went directly to their stalls, Bullet in the left stall, Abby in the middle, and Sox on the right. Once they were in and eating, I went into each stall and put their halters on. Each halter was attached to a clip in the stall by a short lead rope. Once they were all in their stalls, haltered up and eating, I went about the rest of my morning chores.

One morning I had arrived at the barn before the old man and was about ten minutes into my morning routine, when he pulled up in his old truck. I happened to be walking past the front of the barn, so I waited as he climbed out and came over.

"Everything all right today?" he asked, lighting probably his twentieth cigarette of the day.

"Yup," I replied. "Just finishing up with the feeding."

He nodded and turned for the tack room.

"That mare is finished up with her oats, there in the barn," he said nonchalantly. "You should probably turn her out before she causes a ruckus with them geldings."

Now, when the old man pulled into the yard that morning, he stopped his truck nearly thirty feet from the barn where those old horses were eating. He hadn't gone into the barn, and he couldn't see into it either. Yet, somehow he knew one of the horses inside the barn had finished eating. Not only that, but he knew exactly which one. It was almost as if he had x-ray vision.

I went back into the barn, and sure enough, Abby had finished her oats and was trying to get her head into the other two stalls in hopes of stealing a little grain from the geldings. It was a little spooky the way the old man was able to do things like that. Over and over again, he would surprise me by somehow knowing about something that was happening, even when it seemed unlikely that he could have seen or heard it.

The more I thought about what he'd done that morning, the more it bugged me. Unable to stand it any longer, along about noon I approached him and asked him how he knew that the old mare had finished eating.

"By the way it sounded," he said, matter-of-factly.

"By the way what sounded?" I questioned.

"The three feed boxes in them stalls are all different sizes," he explained. "The box in Sox's stall is about eleven inches deep. It used to be twelve, but horses chewed the sides down a bit over the years. It has a sort of low echo when a horse eats out of it. Bullet's box is about eight or nine inches deep, so the echo from it is a little higher pitched."

He mashed the cigarette he was smoking out on the bottom of his boot.

"The box in Abby's stall, now that one's pretty shallow." He rubbed the remaining paper from his cigarette between his fingers until the last of the tobacco filtered out onto the ground. "I doubt it's more than four or five inches deep, at most. It has the highest-pitched echo of the bunch. When I got out of the truck I could hear the two low-pitched echoes, but not the high-pitched one. No echo from a feed box means the horse eatin' outta that box ain't eatin' no more."

I thought he was just pulling my leg. I never noticed the boxes in those stalls being different sizes, and I sure as heck didn't think they made different sounds when horses ate out of them. Even if they did, how was he able to hear the difference standing thirty feet away, outside the building?

Well, rather than asking him to give me a different explanation or elaborate on the one he'd given me, I just let it drop. The next day, however, when I went to put oats in the feed boxes for the three old horses, I took a good look at the boxes, and sure enough, they were all different sizes, just as the old man described. In fact, the feed box in every tie stall in the barn was a slightly different size.

After I let the trio into the barn, I took a few minutes to listen to the sound each box made when the horses ate out of them, and indeed, each one had a slightly different tone. At first the sound of each individual box was indiscernible from the others. But as I listened more closely, Sox's box definitely had the deepest echo, Bullet's was the next deepest, and Abby's had a considerably higher-pitched sound.

So that part of the old man's explanation was true. That still didn't explain how he was able to hear the sounds from thirty feet away, standing outside the barn. As an experiment, I walked slowly out the barn door, paying close attention to how far I could walk away from the barn and still hear the horses eating. By concentrating just on the feed-box sounds, I was actually able to get quite a distance from the barn, perhaps thirty-five or forty feet, and still hear them.

Of course, the farther away I got, the softer and more muddled the sounds became, but that didn't change the fact that I was surprised at how easy the feed-box sounds were to hear, now that I'd paid attention to them. Just the day before I hadn't known those sounds existed, and now they were just about the only thing I could hear! My level of awareness, at least when it came to those sounds, had suddenly and dramatically increased.

From that point forward, I spent a great deal of time listening more closely to the sounds of my surroundings, no matter where I was. I was amazed at how much information I was able to take in just by listening to what was going on around me. Among other things, I learned that each gate on the old man's place made a different sound when it opened and closed. The tack room floor creaked, but only in one spot near the door. The hand pump at the water tank squeaked when you pulled it up, but not when you pushed it down. Most of all, I learned how to tell when Abby finished her feed before the geldings.

It wouldn't be long, however, before the old man, in his understated way, helped me realize that becoming more aware of the sounds around me was only one small part of developing what I would later come to understand as true overall awareness. There were still some senses I needed to engage more fully before that would happen.

This fact became clear when I was riding a little mare out in the back pasture and struggling to get some good forward movement from her. After a while the old man came out and started talking with me about what was going on. He was trying to explain that riding horses should be like floating down a smooth-flowing stream in a canoe, not like trying to push a rope up a hill (which was apparently what it looked like I was trying to do). Then as I sat there on the mare listening to him, he did it again . . .

"The flow I'm talking about," he said, "is like the way that hawk up there lands in that tree. See how she floats onto the branch? No choppy movements."

Now here's the spooky part. The hawk he was referring to was gliding into the top of a tree some fifty yards away and somewhat behind the old man to his left. I could see the bird very clearly as I was facing the old man while he talked, but it seemed impossible that he could see it at the angle he was in relation to the tree.

"How did you know that hawk was landing up there?" I asked in astonishment.

The old man threw a quick glance over his shoulder at the bird, now perched near the top of the tree, and smiled.

"You don't need to be looking directly at something," he said, turning back to me, "to be able to see it."

I had no idea what he was talking about. How could somebody not be looking at something, but see it anyway? It didn't make sense, yet it was apparently possible, since he'd just done that very thing right before my eyes.

A couple of weeks later, after turning a horse out for the night, I was walking along the fence line of the front pasture on my way back to the barn. I was looking at the ground in front of me as I walked, not paying attention to anything in particular, when I suddenly became aware of something off to my right, a movement of some kind out in the pasture.

Like most folks, I suppose, when something caught my eye like that, I would instinctively turn to see what it was. But on that day, for some reason, I chose not to. Instead, I stopped walking but kept looking down at the ground. Then, without looking directly at the pasture, the thing that moved slowly came into view.

The picture I was getting from the far reaches of my peripheral vision was very fuzzy, but the shape was familiar enough for me to recognize it as a small rodent. It was smaller than a rabbit but larger than a mouse. More than likely a ground squirrel or gopher, I concluded. As I stood there looking straight down at the ground, it suddenly became important to me to know which one it was, a ground squirrel or a gopher.

I tried to bring the picture I was getting into a clearer focus without turning my head in the animal's direction, but I just wasn't able to. I stood there, studying the shape and movement of the fuzzy picture I was receiving out of the very corner of my right eye. The color of the animal seemed light brown, almost yellow. Or maybe it was gray. It was hard to get a real good fix on it, because it seemed to change a little each time the animal moved. Its body seemed to be somewhat thick, not like the skinny little gophers we had running around the place. Plus our gophers had a darker brown coat.

Using the little bit of information filtering in, coupled with a few seconds of deductive reasoning, I came to the conclusion the animal must be a ground squirrel, not a gopher. Only after making that decision did I finally turn to see if I was correct.

You can imagine my surprise. Not only was I correct about it being a ground squirrel, but the little guy was actually quite a distance away, about forty-five or fifty feet, and also slightly behind me! Had it not happened to me, I'm not sure I would have believed it. But there it was—I'd been able to see something without looking directly at it, just as the old man had said.

Discovering subtle layers of awareness in these two areas put me on a mission to make both senses, sight and hearing, as good as they could possibly be. Over the years I have spent countless hours developing my vision, specifically my peripheral vision, as well as countless hours improving my ability to hear and distinguish all kinds of different sounds.

I bring up these two examples because I believe they were my initial foray into the world of what I now refer to as true awareness.

Now, I'm certainly not talking about developing supernatural powers or anything like that. Rather, I'm talking about finding a way to awaken abilities we may have inadvertently shut down over the years and enhancing our senses of sight, sound, smell, and touch, with the purpose of learning to use them to their full potential.

A tremendous number of horse-training tools have been invented over the years, all of which seem to be designed to help us achieve better communication with our horses. With my sheltered background, it was quite a shock to see just how many tools you supposedly need to be able to work with horses.

As a kid, the tools we used were basically a halter and lead rope, a saddle, pad, and bridle, and sometimes a pair of thirty-foot driving lines. That was about it. I was amazed to see all these specialized tools, once I got into the "real world" of the horse industry. It seemed there was a tool for every problem, issue, or situation you might possibly encounter with a horse.

Of course, what we often fail to realize is that by using these tools on a regular basis, we have a tendency to rely less and less on the real tools that truly do us the most good—our own minds and bodies.

My theory is that the only reason we need so many tools for working with horses is because we're so bad at using our own minds and bodies in an efficient and productive manner. Rather than working on improving the way we use ourselves, we just take a shortcut via the use of some kind of tool.

I have come to understand that if we're more *aware* of our own bodies and how to use them properly in relationship to how horses use theirs, we find we don't need many of the training tools that are on the market today. Although this has always been a fundamental belief of mine at one level or another, it is certainly something I've given a lot more thought to since beginning my work in martial arts.

Our minds and bodies can be extremely powerful tools when we use them to their maximum potential. The problem comes when we think we've reached that potential or, worse yet, when we give up on trying to achieve our potential. For example, even though I was in pretty bad shape physically prior to beginning my aikido training, I still felt I had good balance, feel, and timing. What I found out very quickly was that they actually left *a lot* to be desired.

I was far from reaching my maximum potential in those areas, but I hadn't given it much thought because my horse work seemed to be going along pretty well. In fact, on a number of levels, the work actually *was* going along pretty well. It just wasn't going along as well as it could have. There were things in my work that I wanted to do better, but I was having a hard time accomplishing them because I was falling short of my own potential.

It wasn't long after I began my aikido training that I had to face the reality of just how far from my potential in those areas I really was. People who were at my same level in class didn't seem to have nearly as much trouble with their balance, feel, and timing as I did. At first, this was extremely hard for me to take and for a while there, I was actually in denial about it. But then a couple of things happened that sort of nudged me along a more positive path and allowed me to begin to make some good progress.

One of those things was that within a couple of months I realized I was spending a lot of time comparing my work to the work of others in class. Coming to this realization was extremely important for me, because a major part of aikido is developing the ability to work on the betterment of yourself without allowing outside distractions to influence you.

Once I came to the realization that I was more concerned with what others were doing than what I was doing, I made a more concerted effort to focus only on my own work, marking my progress by how I felt while performing a certain move, not how I thought someone else looked doing it.

The second, more important thing I did was to begin improving my balance and timing by practicing moves and techniques at home. Prior to that time, I had only practiced in class, as I admittedly felt a little self-conscious performing the dance-like *kata* and other moves at home where someone in my family might actually see me.

After a while, I slowly saw some improvement in my balance, feel, and timing, and I began to look forward to my at-home practice. There were even some days when I found myself working for an hour or two at a time on the same move, performing it over and over again, until it felt exactly the way I wanted it to feel. The next day I would pick a different move or technique and perform it until it felt just right. During these practice sessions, as well as my work in class, I slowly became much more aware of how my body moved and how certain muscles operated in conjunction with others.

With my increased awareness of how my body was meant to operate as a unit, came better feel, timing, and balance. With better feel, timing, and balance came more agility and speed. With agility and speed came a truer understanding of the old saying, "Be quick, but don't hurry." In other words, I gained the ability to perform with speed and precision, as opposed to being fast and sloppy.

Finally, I started to understand how to develop the ability to control the distribution of my weight to different parts of my body and how that affected the outcome of certain moves. For that matter, just understanding that I *could* distribute my weight into different parts of my body was a major eye opener for me!

It was much like learning about the untapped potential of my sight and hearing all those years ago when I was a kid. But this time, I was beginning to feel and understand the previously untapped potential of my own mind and body. When it gets right down to it, our minds and bodies are really the only tools we have available to us all the time, and they're the only ones we don't have to spend a dime to acquire!

Awareness is one of those intangibles we all have available to us, but it is something that takes practice in order to develop, pretty much like everything else worth having. However, people have the tendency to fall into comfortable patterns in their daily lives, and if developing an increased awareness of the world isn't part of those patterns, it can be a hard concept to comprehend, much less try to develop.

I've had people come to clinics over the years who told me they were really struggling with their feel and timing when working with their horses. As a result, they were having a lot of trouble communicating with them in a productive way. During their sessions, I'd try to point out to them when their horses were offering up a "try" or response to their requests. For whatever reason, the owners often weren't able to see or feel it. In some cases, the owners did develop a little better feel—or awareness. In other cases, unfortunately, folks went away not much better off than when we started.

Sometimes I'd hear later they had turned to a method known as "clicker training" to help their horses. In fact, I saw one such rider about a year after we worked with her in one of our clinics. She brought her gelding to the venue where I was working so she could show me the results she was getting using the clicker.

As she went through the exercises she and her horse had been working on using the clicker, I noticed the woman's awareness and timing had improved dramatically. Each time she requested something of her horse and the horse offered up a "try," she was right there with a click and a treat to let the horse know he'd done the right thing. The horse seemed happy in his work, and the owner was very proud.

The longer I watched her work, however, the more I realized the horse wasn't offering any different behavior than we'd seen in the clinic just a year before. He was still responding to her requests in the same way. The big difference was that she was now able to see the responses. The clicker, a tool in this case, apparently helped the woman perceive something she couldn't before.

"Wow, that's great," I said, genuinely impressed with her improvement.

The woman was so intensely focused on her horse that I don't believe she heard me. By that time, the woman was standing in the middle of the round pen and her horse was standing near the rail. She had tossed a small orange cone in that direction, and he had just gone there to touch it with his nose. As he touched it, she gave two short "clicks" with the little child's toy she held in her hand. (We used to call them crickets, when we were kids.) The horse snapped to attention, looked directly at her, and then trotted over, ears erect and giving a soft nicker as he reached her.

"I can't believe I've finally found a training technique *he* likes!" she smiled.

"Yes," I repeated. "That's great."

In the end, it doesn't really matter how we develop our awareness, just that we do. In this case, the woman wasn't able to focus well enough on her own to develop the awareness she needed to reward her horse when he tried to do what she requested. But as soon as she picked up the clicker, all that changed. Having that clicker in her hand gave her the ability to see responses from her horse she wasn't able to see before, even though those responses *were* there long before she had the clicker.

The good news is that she was able to help her horse (and herself, for that matter) over a difficult problem the two of them were having. The bad news is that she was so focused she was effectively shutting out the rest of the world while she did it.

As I see it, there are two kinds of focus that we use in our daily lives. The first is what I call controlled focus, where you can be engrossed in one activity but are also aware of other things happening around you. It's the kind of focus that allows you to drive a car and carry on an intelligent conversation with your friend in the passenger seat at the same time. When you use this kind of focus, you can accomplish two things at once without either being a detriment to the other. You are able to maintain awareness of many things happening around you at once, such as people walking down the street, street signs, store signs, and the clouds rolling overhead.

The second type of focus, however, is what I refer to as uncontrolled focus. That is, you concentrate so intensely on one thing that you are no longer aware of anything else around you. You may be driving your car and talking to your friend in the passenger seat, when suddenly a car in the oncoming lane swerves into your lane. Immediately all your focus and attention goes straight to that car. Suddenly you can't see anything else and you can't even hear your friend yell a warning!

The uncontrolled focus in this second scenario, according to recent studies, is now known to be one of the biggest causes of accidents that are potentially preventable. A driver sees a car crossing the centerline and coming toward him in his lane. Instead of looking for a way to avoid hitting the oncoming car, the driver gets tunnel vision, focuses totally on the oncoming car, and simply drives straight into it, causing a head-on collision.

We all experience uncontrolled focus at one time or another. We concentrate so hard on something we're working on or somebody we're talking to that everything else around us seems to disappear.

A number of years ago I was working with a new gelding that was pretty sticky backing up. He'd take a couple very stiff steps backward when I asked, but then he'd stop. The horse's previous owner told me that the horse had been backing like that for as long as he'd had him, three years.

After a few minutes I was able to get the gelding's feet freed up, and he was backing much softer. However, I very quickly noticed that even though he was backing more freely, he was going pretty crooked. In fact, he was so crooked that every time we finished backing, we were facing a completely different direction. Once, we got so far off track that when we started backing we were facing east, and when we finished backing, we were facing west!

Every time I asked the horse to back up, I made a very conscious effort to remain aware of how straight he was. As soon as I caught him going crooked, I immediately put a leg on him to straighten him up. Unfortunately, any time I put a leg on him, I inadvertently overcorrected him, and I wound up putting my opposing leg on him to fix it. Before long I was alternating legs on him just to try and keep him straight. Not surprisingly, he became confused, and within a very short time, he went right back to having sticky feet when he backed.

As you can imagine, it became quite a dilemma for me—not to mention how the horse must have felt—and it was a week-and-a-half before I finally stumbled on a solution. I had just climbed into the saddle and was getting ready to ask the gelding to back, when I heard one of my wranglers off in the distance.

"Wow, did you see that!" she exclaimed.

My head immediately popped up to see what she was looking at. Across the valley, nearly a half-mile away, a momma black bear with a pair of cubs had emerged briefly from the woods and then headed back the way they'd came. I watched until they disappeared into the trees and then turned my attention back to what I was doing. It was then that it suddenly occurred to me what the problem had been all along. As I said, when I heard the wrangler yell, my head popped up to see who was causing all the ruckus. And there it was . . . in order for my head to pop *up*, it must first have been *down!*

Sure enough, every time I asked the horse to back up, I started by looking straight down at the back of his head. Even before I picked up the reins to ask him to back, my head and eyes would drop. I became so focused on the back of the gelding's head that I wasn't able to see anything else around me.

While I backed the gelding, I fell into a form of uncontrolled focus, just as the woman using the clicker had. In her case, it worked out in a mostly beneficial way; for me it wasn't working out very well at all. I was looking down at my horse's head and developing such tunnel vision that I lost sight of where we were and where we were going. I was backing him crooked and then trying to fix it after it was already a problem—a problem, by the way, that I was causing because I wasn't paying attention.

Once I figured out what I was doing, I kept my head up, looked at a target out in front of us, and then asked him to back. By doing so, I became much more aware of where we were in relation to where we started and much more aware of everything around us while we performed our task. If he got a little crooked, instead of fixing him with my legs, I simply kept his head, as well as mine, facing the target. After backing him this way only four or five times, the crookedness went away completely.

In my opinion, the key to true awareness is the ability to focus on one thing, while maintaining awareness of all the other things around you at the same time. It takes a lot of practice and work to become good at it. But the hardest part is trying to find a way to get started.

Most of us approach our horses after a long day at the office and expect to be aware enough to be able to pick up on every (or nearly every) subtle movement, shift of weight, or change of attitude they exhibit. The truth is, most of the time we aren't even aware of the subtle movements, shifts of weight, or changes of attitude that we make throughout the day, so it's no wonder we struggle finding those things in our horses.

I think what we sometimes fail to realize that awareness doesn't start when we go to work with our horses. It starts when we wake up in the morning, and it's something we take to our horses. In my opinion, that is really the only way we can consistently remain truly aware, day in and day out.

How do you work on improving awareness on a daily basis? Well, I think that differs from one person to the next. I suppose if it were me, I'd begin by trying to be more aware of what it takes to perform simple tasks, the tasks I do every day without giving them a second thought.

I might start with something as simple as getting out of bed. What does it take to roll out of bed and put my feet on the floor? What muscles do I use to stand up? What does it take for me to brush my teeth, eat breakfast, pull on my boots, or sit in a chair? How, exactly, do I get out of a chair, pick up the telephone, or turn on the shower? And we haven't even left the house yet!

Several years ago, even prior to my training in aikido, I decided I wanted to become more aware of everything I did, and everything around me. Without knowing how to go about it, I decided to begin just as I've explained. I chose one simple task every day and studied it. Each day it was a different task, something I would just pick out of the blue. One day it was putting the saddle on my horse's back, the next day it might be putting on my socks. I studied how I put my hat on and how I took it off. I studied what it took to open my truck door and what it took to put on my chaps. I studied how I picked up my guitar, and the muscles it took to hold and play it. I studied the movements it took to accomplish each task, the muscles it involved, how much effort each task required. In the end, I became aware of the simple things I did every day.

It was an interesting experiment for me (and it's something I continue to do to this day), because the more I became aware of my own activities, the more aware I became of everything else around me—the sounds, sights, and smells of things I hadn't noticed before.

Not long ago I was having lunch with my assistant, Kathleen, at one of our week-long clinics in Loveland, Colorado. We were sitting in a couple of chairs inside a large, open-ended shed. My wife, Wendy, was supposed to meet us for lunch that day, but she had called to say she was running late. She wasn't sure when she'd be there and asked us not to wait for her.

At any rate, Kathleen and I were eating and talking over some things we'd worked on with the riders from the morning when suddenly I picked up on a familiar sound coming from the road, perhaps a half-mile away.

"It sounds like Wendy's coming," I said to Kathleen.

"What do you mean?" she asked.

"I hear her coming down the road."

Kathleen sat quietly for a few seconds.

"I don't hear anything," she shrugged. Several more seconds passed.

"She's getting ready to turn in the driveway." I nodded my head toward one end of the shed.

From where we were sitting, we couldn't see the road or the driveway to the ranch, but I didn't have to see our little Ford Ranger to know Wendy had just arrived. The sounds of that truck's tires on the pavement, and the sounds they made as they hit the driveway stones were very distinctive to me, although I hadn't really ever given it much thought until right that minute. Regardless, I knew it was Wendy in our truck.

"Get outta here," Kathleen chuckled. "I don't hear any . . ."

Just then Wendy pulled around the corner and parked the little white pickup near the round pen, in full view of us. Kathleen watched as Wendy climbed out of the truck and then turned back to me and smiled.

I believe perhaps the single most important asset a horseperson can have is the ability to know and understand what the horse is offering in response to cues and how other things around the horse might motivate it in a positive or negative way. In other words, the more aware we are, the better our chances are of being able to communicate with horses (or other people, for that matter) in a productive way.

When I look back to my time with the old man all those years ago, I can see just how high his level of awareness was. The responses he got from horses, using cues that seemed imperceptible, used to boggle my mind. I don't know how many times I walked away after watching him work with a horse, mumbling to myself, "How'd he do that?"

Well, now I believe I have an idea. He was able to accomplish those amazing things because he had the ability to see things I couldn't see, hear things I couldn't hear, and feel things I couldn't feel. His ability to do those things was the result of a lifetime of quiet and persistent practice.

At the time, I thought I would never get to that level, and I still may not. But at least now I have an idea about where to look . . . and listen . . . and feel.

10

Commitment

It didn't happen very often—maybe only once or twice a year—that the old man would just come up to me out of the blue and tell me to saddle up because we were going for a ride together. I always enjoyed those rides. They were not only a great distraction from my long list of daily chores, they also got me on a horse. Any chance I had to ride was a bonus in my eyes, pure and simple.

On this particular day, the old man decided we'd ride first thing in the morning. As soon as I'd finished feeding and cleaning, we each picked a horse from the field, saddled up, and headed out through the back pasture. From there, we rode the trail that wound its way through the woods. That trail branched off into a number of other trails, and depending on which paths we chose, we might be away from the barn an hour or a half-day or more.

Our ride that day turned out to be one of the longer ones. We left the barn at about 9:30 and didn't start heading back until just after noon. It was a great ride, very quiet and relaxing. When we went on these rides, it was often because the old man had something he wanted to talk to me about, maybe about the work I was doing, but not on this ride. Neither one of us said a whole lot, other than when the old man pointed out a deer grazing in a clearing and when I asked him a question about a horse back at the barn. My question was more of a feeble attempt at starting a conversation than it was my wanting an answer, and I guess the old man knew it, because he gave me a pretty feeble reply in return. I realized then that this was a day for riding, not a day for talking.

After a while, I just sort of relaxed into the rhythm of my horse's movements and began simply to enjoy the ride. We made a huge loop out, and by the time we turned back, we had ridden nearly six miles from the barn. We were only a mile or so away from the barn when we turned onto a small, rarely traveled part of the trail that ran parallel to a small stream that we'd eventually need to cross.

Admittedly, my mind had been wandering aimlessly from one unsubstantial thought to another for the better part of an hour, and as a result, I'd given little thought to Dixie, the older mare I was riding. Dixie was one of those "bombproof" horses. She was as steady as they come and honest as the day is long, and for the most part, if you pointed her nose down the trail, she would just keep going until you asked her to do something different. It was for those very reasons I chose to ride Dixie. I figured riding her would be easy, and I sure didn't feel like training some young horse for three hours, when all we wanted to do was go for a trail ride.

At any rate, we had only been riding along the stream for few minutes when suddenly a small flock of ducks took off from the stream bank closest to us. They had evidently been feeding so close to the bank that none of us saw or heard them, and when they took off, they really made one heck of a ruckus, quacking loudly and splashing water everywhere.

Much to my surprise, the first thing Dixie (you know, the bombproof, rock-solid, steady-as-they-come older mare that would be easier to ride than some young colt) did was spook. She jumped off to the right side of the trail and landed right in the middle of a wild rose bush. Evidently, landing in that bush was very uncomfortable, and Dixie threw in a halfhearted buck, jumping back out of the bush and across the trail toward the stream.

This buck very effectively dislodged me from the saddle, and as I scrambled to regain my balance, Dixie suddenly realized she was heading straight for the stream and was only a few feet away from it. Well, I'm guessing she didn't want to get herself wet, because just a second before she reached the stream bank, she very abruptly veered to the right to avoid falling in. Unfortunately for me, at that moment I just happened to be hanging precariously off the left side of the saddle, halfway between coming off her back and staying on, and that turn to the right was just enough to finish the job.

Thankfully, I landed on my back in a soft, grassy spot on the very edge of the bank, and I probably would have been all right had I not rolled slightly when I hit. I rolled on a very loose spot in the bank, causing a three-foot section of the bank to give way and sending me face first down toward the slow-moving stream.

I immediately tried to push myself back up the bank, working frantically to keep my head and upper body out of the water, but the more I pushed, the more the bank gave way. I pulled desperately backwards with my knees and pushed up with my hands, but it was no use. After a monumental struggle that lasted all of about thirty seconds, the fruitlessness of my efforts became apparent and I resigned myself to the fact I was going to get wet. I stopped fighting and slid haplessly into the water.

The water in the stream wasn't all that deep, but it was deep enough to get me pretty wet as I thrashed around on the muddy bottom trying to get back on my feet. When I finally did, I turned to see Dixie standing only a few yards from where I had come off, grazing peacefully, as if nothing had happened. The old man, who had been behind me when the ducks took flight and all hell broke loose, was sitting on his horse, calmly smiling.

"You shoulda kept riding," he said, looking down at me.

"What do you mean by that?" I shot back, as I tried to crawl up the still-collapsing bank. "I was riding! It ain't my fault she decided to buck me off!"

"She didn't buck you off." His voice had a hint of bluntness to it. "You fell off 'cuz you quit riding."

"What are you talking about?" I asked, obviously upset. "I *was* riding."

"No," he corrected me. "You *weren't* riding. You were *sitting*. You quit *riding* over an hour ago."

He rode over to Dixie, reached down, and took hold of her reins. Then he started ponying her down the trail toward the barn. At first I figured he was just moving her to a more level spot to make it easier for me to get back on, but I quickly realized that wasn't the case at all. He was taking my horse and heading back home.

"You can go ahead and walk the rest of the way," he said, without looking back at me. "That backside of yours is too wet and muddy to be in one of my good saddles."

I stood there, looking like a drowned rat, as he rode away.

"It ain't that far," he continued, raising his voice a little as the distance between us increased. "Maybe you'll be dried off by the time you get back."

I had no idea what the old man meant when he told me I'd fallen off Dixie because I quit riding, and the mile or so walk back to the barn did absolutely nothing to clear up my confusion. From my perspective as a young kid, I couldn't see how you could be on a horse as it moved and not be riding it. It didn't make any sense at all.

Even though I had absolutely no idea what he was talking about at the time, his statement about "not riding" stuck with me.

It was a pretty nice day—as are many autumn days in the Rocky Mountains—warm and sunny, with just the hint of a breeze. It was midafternoon, and I happened to be driving by the local rodeo grounds when I noticed a number of horse trailers in the parking lot. I knew the rodeo and horse-show season was over, so just out of curiosity, I decided to stop in and see what was going on.

It turns out members of the local saddle club were all there having a family "fun day" with their horses. As I slowly drove through the parking lot, I could see that the activities were already wrapping up, and for the most part the folks who were still there were just sitting around talking. Some of them were on horses, others were sitting in folding chairs, and still others were standing in small circles, all seemingly going over the day's activities.

Seeing as how all the riding was finished, I decided to head for home. I swung the truck around in a big open space at the end of the parking lot and started back the way I'd come, when something off to my right caught my eye. I turned to see a young gal, maybe in her late teens, galloping a sorrel quarter horse across a small, open field not far from where I was. In front of her, maybe 200 yards away, was a group of people on horseback moving lazily along at a walk.

As I watched the girl on the quarter horse close on the group of riders, I noticed a couple of the horses in the group get a little antsy. Nothing major . . . just a few heads popping up in an attempt to see what was coming behind them. When the quarter horse flew past, three of the horses from the group tried to go along with it. Two of the riders were successful in getting their horses to settle back down, but the third was obviously having a little more trouble.

The rider pulled hard on the reins as his horse lunged forward, causing the horse's head to fly dramatically upward as his front feet left the ground. The rider immediately put his hands forward on the horse's neck, releasing the pressure on the reins and causing the horse to sort of pirouette on his hind feet and land hard on his front feet facing the group of riders. The rider fell over the horse's neck. Then, as the horse jumped forward toward the other horses, the rider was pitched backward.

The horse did a sort of half-buck, half-jump, and even though the rider was off balance, he still seemed to handle it with very little trouble. Then the horse took three more of those jumps forward. With the first jump, it was obvious the rider was trying hard to regain his balance in the saddle. At the second jump, the rider was losing his seat a little, but it was clear he was still in good shape as far as being able to stay on.

As I watched from my truck, I was as sure as I could be that the rider wasn't going to come off. After all, the movement of the horse wasn't all that bad, and the fellow on his back seemed to be a pretty fair rider, so there was no reason to think the situation would end badly for either one of them.

Then it happened. It was the first time I'd really seen it firsthand. Sure enough, though, there it was. Somewhere between the horse's second and third jump, the rider simply stopped riding. Even from where I was, nearly a quarter-mile from the action, it was plain to see he just "went away," both mentally and physically, and gave up trying to help himself or the horse. By the time the fourth jump came, the rider toppled over the horse's right shoulder in a rather harmless, albeit unceremonious, manner and came to rest on his backside on the ground.

The look that fellow had when he stopped riding was amazing. It was as if someone had flipped a switch. He went from being an active, determined rider trying to control the situation to little more than a bewildered passenger looking for a place to hit the ground. His entire body took on the look of someone who had resigned himself to the fact that he wasn't going to be able to stay on, even though it looked for the world as though he could have easily brought everything to a quiet conclusion . . . had he just kept *riding*.

Since that day the old man told me *I* had quit riding (when I was as sure as I could be that I hadn't), I had given the idea quite a bit of thought, trying to figure out exactly what he meant. Over the years I'd come to realize he wasn't one of those men who talked just to hear the sound of his own voice. No, if he said something, there was a reason for it, and more times than not, it was a very good reason.

Knowing that, the question of what it meant to "quit riding" would just pop into my head from time to time, rumble around for a few days, and then slowly fade out without being resolved. However, once I saw what it meant for someone to quit riding, I found the idea became such an important concept that it shaped my work in ways I couldn't have even imagined at the time.

Since the "fun day" at the rodeo grounds, I have become much more aware of what it looks like to quit riding, as well as what it feels like when it happens. I have come to realize that what we're talking about here isn't so much the act of a person who quits riding, per se, as it is the act of a person not riding in the first place.

What happened to me that day the old man and I were out riding is a good case in point. We'd been out on the trail all morning and into the afternoon. By the time we were heading back to the barn, I had gone from an active participant in the ride to little more than a passenger on my horse. I remember distinctly that I had been daydreaming, lazily watching the scenery go by, and swaying mindlessly to the steady rhythm of Dixie's movement, as she put one foot in front of the other in her march back home.

The old man had been right. I quit riding my horse long before she spooked and I fell off. I had pretty much detached myself from the entire situation hours before those ducks flew, so when Dixie spooked, there was no way I could get myself in a position, either mentally or physically, to do either one of us any good. I was still riding *on* Dixie when the wheels fell off, but I most certainly wasn't riding *with* her. And that, in and of itself, is the difference.

If we're going to be of any use at all to our horses, we need to learn how to ride *all the time*, not just when it's convenient for us. How many of us can look at our last ride, for instance, and truly say we were right there, in the moment, with our horses the entire time we were on their backs?

My guess is that if we take a long hard look at how we ride our horses, what we might find is that if we're on our horses' backs for an hour, we might only be riding on average for about twenty minutes out of that hour. The rest of the time we're thinking about what we're going to have for supper or the best route to take to work the next day or when to make an appointment to have the oil changed or what should go on our grocery list or how to handle the barking dog across the road or how our kid's grades in school are coming along—any number of thoughts that are completely insignificant to our horse and have nothing to do with riding!

In the meantime, we have effectively become little more than a passenger on our horse's back, while the horse, on the other hand, continues to keep working. By the time we get off our horse after our one-hour ride, we have *not* ridden for forty minutes.

Now this is a very important piece of the puzzle, because as pretty much everybody knows, the more you practice something, the better at it you become. Because so many of us ride without intent or awareness much of the time we're on our horses, we inadvertently spend that time practicing how *not* to ride, so when something unforeseen happens, such as our horse spooking, we end up being caught completely off guard. We instinctively fall back on the skills we have been practicing—not riding. And we all know what happens next.

Now I'm sure there are some folks out there saying, "Hey, what's this guy talking about? I ride my horse to relax. I like looking at the trees, listening to the birds, and visiting with the friends I ride with. I don't want to have to be so focused on my horse that I can't enjoy the ride, for crying out loud!"

And you know what . . . I agree. I'm not talking about taking the fun out of riding here. Rather, I'm talking about making an effort to be aware of your horse's movements and actions while you ride, instead of taking a mental trip to Ireland as he carries you up and down the trail. I'm talking about having at least the same amount of awareness when you are on your horse that you have when you drive your car (or, in some cases, maybe a little more).

Much of the trouble folks have with their horses usually boils down to one of two things. Either it is a lack of knowledge on the owner's part (a "yellow belt" owner trying to do "black belt" things with his horse) or it is a lack of commitment in the way the owner rides or handles his horse. In other words, we may start riding one way—with purpose and intent. But as we finish the trail ride, we may be riding in a completely different manner, perhaps with indifference or a lack of purpose and intent. We end up going from one end of the spectrum to the other, often within little more than an hour's time. Then we wonder why our horses tend to get a little spooky on the trail, why they can't seem to hold their attention on us, or why they can't seem to focus on the task at hand. Yet, in each case, the problem can usually be traced back to the rider's lack of commitment, not the horse's lack of effort.

In my opinion, between the two—a lack of knowledge or a lack of commitment—it is a rider's lack of commitment that is actually the more perilous. With a lack of commitment, the rider usually has the proper knowledge of what he is trying to accomplish, but doesn't use that knowledge in a productive way, at the right time, or in the right manner.

Every minute we are with our horses, whether on their backs or working with them on the ground, is a minute we could be using to practice our awareness and communication. By practicing those things all the time, we automatically tend to become more committed. However, if we choose not to practice those qualities, then we shouldn't be surprised when our horses do something that takes us by surprise!

I have given this idea of commitment—or riding all the time, if you will—a great deal of thought over the years. I have spent a lot of time trying to work on being as committed to the task at hand as possible, as well as on improving consistency with my horses and in the work I do. Up until just a few years ago, I felt this was an area of my life that I had a pretty good handle on. That is, until I began my work in aikido.

About a year had passed since I began my aikido training, and during that time, there hadn't been any tests for students for advancement to the next rank. So a number of other students, including myself, had remained at a white-belt ranking, the level we all held from the very first day.

The time frame for ranking tests generally depends on the skill level of the students. The lower the rank, the sooner they are allowed to test. For the most part, this is due to the amount of knowledge required to move ahead. Normally a lower-ranking student might test every three or four months.

I told myself, from the beginning, that the color of the belt I had shouldn't really make all that much difference. I was in the class to help improve my horsemanship and nothing more. So, after being a white belt for a year, testing wasn't that big of a deal for me. Or so I thought.

Our first test was to be held at 6:30 on a Tuesday evening during one of our regular classes. Throughout the day, I felt like everything went along pretty much like any other day. I went about my chores and the rest of my business without giving the impending test that much thought. Around 5:00, I got together with my two young sons, Tyler and Aaron (both of whom were also testing in aikido that night), and we just sort of walked through the techniques we would be tested on. Everything seemed to go pretty well, and I felt none of us had much to worry about.

But as 6:30 got closer, something strange began to happen. Out of the blue I started feeling a few butterflies in my stomach. I had no idea why, because I thought I felt pretty confident about my abilities and the techniques. Yet when I got my *gi* out of the closet and began getting dressed, I noticed that not only did I still have the butterflies, the palms of my hands were a little sweaty, too. Driving to the dojo, I started running through all the techniques I would be tested on in my mind, and much to my chagrin, found I could only remember one out of the five or six I'd been practicing for the last year.

When we got to the dojo, a number of us nervously joked around while we waited for the tai chi class to end. Still, the butterflies remained, and my nervousness seemed to be amplified to some degree. Tai chi finally ended, and as the students left the floor, each of them shook our hands and wished us well. That made me feel a little better, but not much.

As our class started, I found almost right away I was struggling. My *kata*, the first thing I learned when I began my training, seemed completely foreign to me, almost as though I'd never performed it before. My foot and hand placements were off, and my movements were slow and choppy, instead of smooth and flowing.

As we went through the basics, I found I had trouble remembering the names of the techniques and how to perform them. Sensei Marty and Shihan Adams came up to me from time to time and reviewed the things I was supposed to know—and thought I did—talking with me like it was the first time I'd ever seen or performed the techniques. I felt embarrassed. The class seemed to drag on forever, and everything I tried to perform required a major effort on my part.

Finally, the class wound down, and our teachers, Sensei Marty, Sensei Jo, and Shihan Adams, went into another room to do the grading. I stood there in line with the other students feeling as though I had completely failed my first-ever martial arts test. Of course, standing there in line, I had no trouble remembering the names of all the techniques or the moves used to perform them. But I was as sure as I could be that it was too late.

A few minutes later, our three instructors emerged with the results of the test. Much to my surprise, I hadn't failed after all. Not only did I not fail, but I was one of four students who had advanced from a white belt to a blue belt, skipping two levels (yellow and orange) in between. I think I walked around for the next three days just shaking my head in amazement. But more than that, for those same three days I was completely exhausted, both mentally and physically, and had no idea why.

The next week we all went back to our regular training, and then suddenly four months had gone by and it was time for our next test. Just like the first time, I felt pretty confident about my abilities in the days leading up to it, but a few hours before the test, I began to get a pretty good case of nerves.

As the test began, I quickly started feeling as though it was going to be a carbon copy of the first. I struggled with just about everything asked of me, and I had this overwhelming feeling of total incompetence. By the time the test was over, I was as sure as I could be that I hadn't come anywhere near passing. Yet I had indeed passed and been promoted from a blue belt to a purple belt.

Once again for the three days following the test, I found myself walking around completely exhausted, both mentally and physically. I kept telling myself that there was just no way I should be feeling that bad. After all, while the test was certainly much more rigorous than a regular class, it wasn't so intense that I should be completely worn out for three days. Something wasn't right, and I decided to take a harder look at the situation.

It was funny, because once I made a conscious effort to look at the big picture, it didn't take long to find the root of my problem. I started by going to the next two classes with a whole new attitude.

I made sure I was paying very close attention to every little thing I did in class in hopes it would lead me to an answer, and sure enough, it did.

What I noticed during those two classes was that even though I was physically there in class and doing the work, my mind wandered off at least four or five times per class. And when I say it wandered off, I mean it wandered off. Instead of giving my full attention to the class, I was thinking about the people walking past the window outside, the two visitors who had come to watch the class, the fact that my belt didn't stay tied, or any number of other trivial matters that had nothing at all to do with my work in aikido!

Instead of giving my full attention to the activity I was engaged in, I was spending nearly half my time in class thinking about other things. It doesn't take a rocket scientist to figure out that if I was only spending half my time in class thinking about aikido, then I was, in effect, wasting the other half of class, simply throwing it away! By the time four months passed by, I'd only participated in two months' worth of classes, even though I had physically attended all of them.

That was why I was so worn out, both mentally and physically, following a test. During the test, I was *forced* to remain mentally engaged the entire time. Because I was taking so much time off during my regular classes, I wasn't mentally in shape to do that. As a result, I just played out and wasn't able to give my best. And, to be honest, I didn't even know what my best was!

Well, it didn't take me long to decide *that* was going to have to change. And change it did. By the third class following the test, I had a completely different game plan. I went into that class—and every class after it—as if it were a test day. I consciously made an effort not to take *any* time off, either mentally or physically, from the time I walked into the dojo until the time I walked out. And once I started approaching my work in that way, I began to see amazing improvement.

Not only did the classes become more fun (even though we were learning much more difficult moves and techniques), but I also found it easier to retain the information being presented, no matter which instructor it was coming from or how it was taught. I slowly began to feel my energy level increase, and my breathing and movements became much more focused. I found increased awareness of some of the subtleties of individual techniques, as well as an understanding of their importance in the overall concept of the maneuvers.

By the time our third test rolled around four months later, I finally felt like I was truly ready for it. The case of nerves I had going into the two previous tests never showed up, and as the test began, I actually felt good about what I was doing. As the test progressed, I felt as though I was falling into some sort of "zone," as if I was being picked up and carried through each task, instead of being dragged through it.

Before I knew it, the test was over, and our teachers were all in the next room doing the grading. I stood in line waiting for them to emerge, and this time I found I wasn't concerned with whether I had passed or failed, but instead I just felt very good about the work I'd done. I had done my best from start to finish, and that was all that really mattered.

When our teachers came back out into the dojo and announced the results, I was somewhat shocked to find not only had I been promoted from purple belt to green belt, but I had also been promoted to the "head student" position, as well. Following that promotion, I continued to train as if each class I attended were a test, and each time another test came up, I felt a sort of calm tranquility going into it. I never felt as if I wasn't ready, but by the same token, I wasn't overconfident of my ability or skill level either. I was where I was and whether or not I was promoted was out of my hands once I walked into the test anyway. My teachers would feel I deserved to be promoted or they wouldn't. Either way, I would do my best the entire time I was there and let the chips fall where they may.

In the end, all I had really done to initiate this change in my work was decide to practice my aikido the way I practice my horsemanship. In other words, I would *ride all the time*. I would remain committed to my work. And interestingly enough, the results I received were much the same.

❀

Over the years, I have come to understand that no matter what activity we are engaged in—horsemanship, martial arts, putting up hay, building fence, working in an office, digging a ditch, or whatever—our success is tied directly to the way we practice. The more time we take off mentally while we're performing the activity, the longer it will take to master it, if we master it at all. The more commitment we bring to the activity (the idea of riding all the time), the more success we are likely to have.

I guess we have all heard at one time or another the old saying, "Anything worth doing is worth doing right." I, for one, agree with that wholeheartedly. Unfortunately, in our society it seems we have gotten away from that concept, and mediocrity has become more the norm.

I think what we tend to forget is that we are all capable of great things, each and every one of us. It's just that there aren't any shortcuts that will get us there. But time, hard work, and commitment might.

Staying Centered

The great martial artist Bruce Lee once said during an interview that before he began studying martial arts, he believed a punch was just a punch. He saw it as nothing more than a way to fend off someone who was trying to do harm to another. However, a few years into his martial arts training, he began to see it differently.

As he studied, he became aware of all the angles from which a punch could be thrown. He learned how to form a fist in such a way as to make any punch he threw much more effective. He learned to focus all of his power into one small spot on just one of his knuckles, eventually enabling him to break wooden boards, concrete blocks, and pretty much anything else he set his mind to. He spent years studying the punch, and over time the punch became a symbol of his knowledge, power, control, and achievement.

But then something else happened. The longer he studied martial arts and the more he learned about and understood the punch, the more he began to see that, in the end, a punch was just a punch—nothing more than a way to fend off someone who was trying to do harm to another.

It was early evening on a Saturday in late September, and my friend, Dwight, and I were on our way home to Colorado from a draft-horse sale in Rapid City, South Dakota. We'd purchased three teams of big, black percheron geldings, along with a real nice brood mare in foal. Because our trailer happened to be in the repair shop that weekend, we'd arranged for a friend to transport home any horses we happened to buy. So once we got our new horses loaded into his trailer late that afternoon, Dwight and I were free to leave, and we started for home.

We hadn't gone very far when we realized we hadn't had anything to eat since breakfast, so we stopped at a small bar in Torrington, Wyoming, for a burger. There was a bone-chilling wind blowing out of the northwest, and dark clouds billowed up thousands of feet into the sky. Partly because of the weather and partly because it was Saturday, this watering hole was nearly full by the time we stopped in. Sitting on stools at the bar and in chairs at the tables scattered around the dim, smoky room was a variety of cowboys and cowgirls and ranchers and farmers, as well as a few "city folk," all of whom seemed to know one another.

The only places for us to sit were two stools at the corner of the bar near the wall, right next to a couple of weathered old-timers in crumpled cowboy hats and tattered Carhartt jackets.

"Anybody sittin' here?" Dwight asked, before we took the seats.

"Naw," one of the old timers grunted, "go ahead."

Trying not to be too conspicuous (but not doing a very good job of it), the two old men threw wary glances in our direction as we sat down. They sized us up right away as outsiders, but since we were dressed in old, sweat-stained cowboy hats, faded jackets frayed around the edges, and jeans and boots still spattered with cow manure, they must have decided we were okay. They nonchalantly returned to their conversation.

The activities of the past three days were catching up with Dwight and me. We'd moved cattle all morning two days before and then pretty much got off our horses and drove non-stop to Rapid City, pulling in late that night. After getting up early the next two mornings to attend the sale, we were hurrying home because we had cattle to sort the next day. So, we were pretty tired and pretty quiet as we sat there at the bar waiting for our food.

Our quiet weariness that evening did give us the chance to overhear the old-timers talking about a couple of young horses one of them was starting under saddle. Evidently, one of the colts had been pretty easy to start and was going along fairly well. The other was apparently not as cooperative and had bucked the old man off a couple of times already.

The two of them discussed a number of ideas the old fellow could try to stop the horse from bucking, with nothing really being resolved. After a while and with the conversation apparently at an end, the fellow who'd been working with the colts pushed two quarters and his empty beer glass across the bar.

"Well, I guess I better go," he said, turning on his bar stool and steadying himself on the bar as he got to his feet. "My wife's got supper on."

"Yeah, I better git, too," the other nodded. "I been loafin' long enough fer one day."

He picked up his glass and finished the couple of swallows of beer that had been left in it since before we sat down.

"We'll see ya tomorrow, Ron," the first one said matter-of-factly, as he slowly walked past his friend and patted him on the shoulder.

"Yeah," Ron replied, wiping his mouth with his sleeve as he set his empty glass on the bar. "Keep a leg on each side and yer mind in the middle."

"Yup," the first nodded. "I'll do my best."

It wasn't the first time I'd heard someone use that old phrase: *Keep a leg on each side and your mind in the middle.* And it wouldn't be the last. But it was the first time I'd heard it used "for real." When most modern-day horse folks use that phrase, it's just a folksy way to say good-bye or maybe a joke aimed at a person who might be riding, say, a dead-broke, old trail horse.

But when Ron said it to his old friend in the bar, he actually meant it. I believe he was saying, "No matter what that colt does when you're riding him, keep your mind focused on the task at hand." It was a sort of gentle reminder from one old horseman to another to keep it simple and ride well, even if everything went bad.

Up until then, I'd never really given the old saying much thought, but I sure have since. The idea behind it is a very simple concept. Basically, it's a reminder to keep your "middle" right smack dab in the middle of the horse, because once your middle gets off kilter, things can happen that aren't always in your best interest. Yes, at first glance, it's a simple concept.

However, this concept is so important that it literally makes up the very heart of every discipline, including every style of horsemanship and riding there is throughout the world. Essentially, what we're talking about here is being both physically (*keep a leg on each side*) and mentally (*your mind in the middle*) centered when we ride. Easy to say . . . not always so easy to do.

Strangely, this can be a difficult notion to get our minds around, because many of us have forgotten or never really knew what it means to be centered. As a result, when we try to work on getting ourselves centered in the saddle, we often don't know where to start.

I thought I had an understanding of the concept of being centered years ago, but I can see now that my level of comprehension was just scratching the surface. That's probably why I began having all the trouble I did with my work. You see, anytime we work just on the surface of an activity, no matter what it is, sooner or later we're bound to run into trouble.

After I began my training in martial arts, I gained a truer understanding of the concept of being centered, both physically and mentally. Ironically, the event that really kick-started the idea occurred while I was watching an aikido instructor talk to a group of horse people at a clinic I was doing up in Washington state. At the time, I'd been studying aikido for about a year-and-a-half and was just starting to get a feel for a few of the techniques and methods of the art. Admittedly, I still didn't have a real good understanding of them.

About halfway through his talk, the instructor asked a student from the group to step forward. He then asked if he could lightly touch her forehead with his finger, and she giddily agreed.

"What I would like you to do," he said, as he touched the smiling woman on the forehead, "is think about this particular spot . . .

nothing else . . . just this spot. Try to get all your thoughts right here."

At first, the woman appeared to feel a little foolish, standing in front of a bunch of people with a man's finger touching her forehead. But as the instructor waited quietly, keeping his finger lightly on her forehead, the woman's smile slowly faded and her eyes slowly closed.

"Good," he continued. "Now, tell me when you feel like you've got all your thoughts on this spot."

The woman stood quietly for a few seconds, then slowly nodded her head.

"Okay," the instructor said, as he lowered his hand from her forehead. "Now, I'm going to try to move you by putting my hand on your shoulder and lightly pushing you backward. You try to resist me, but keep your thoughts on that spot on your forehead. Okay?"

Again the woman, eyes still closed, slowly nodded her head. The instructor placed his hand lightly on her shoulder and gave a gentle push. Immediately, the woman, who was obviously trying to resist, started falling backward. The instructor reached up and supported her so she wouldn't fall, and she opened her eyes.

"Okay," he nodded. "That was good. So now let's try this. I want to do the same thing, but this time I would like you to touch yourself right here." He pointed to a spot on his own chest, about the middle of his sternum. The woman took her right hand and touched herself in the same place on her own chest.

"Right here?" she asked.

"Yes, that's it," he said. "Now this time, try to put all your thoughts in that spot and then tell me when you're there."

The woman slowly closed her eyes, pressing her finger lightly into her sternum.

"Okay," she said softly, after a few seconds.

The instructor placed his hand on her shoulder and pushed lightly. The woman seemed much steadier on her feet than before, but still lost her balance and began to tip backward a little.

"Pretty good," the instructor said enthusiastically. "Now let's try one more thing. I'd like you to take that same finger and touch this spot on yourself."

He placed his finger about two inches directly below his belly button. The woman touched the same spot on herself.

"Good," he said. "Now I want you to really think about that spot. Put all your thoughts right where you have your hand."

The woman closed her eyes. She took a deep breath and slowly let it out, causing her entire body to just sort of settle right there where she was standing. She gave a slow but somewhat more determined nod, indicating she was ready, and the instructor reached up and placed his hand on her shoulder.

He started off just as he had before, with a relatively light, steady push. The lady didn't budge. He noticeably increased the pressure, and the woman didn't move. He pushed harder yet and still there was no movement. Finally, he braced against her as though he was trying to push a car out of the mud. There he was, a 200-pound man, pushing against a woman who was five-feet tall and maybe 115 pounds soaking wet. Astonishingly, that little gal stood there like her entire body was somehow anchored to the ground. It was as if he could have tried to push her over with a truck and still wouldn't have been able to move her. It was truly an amazing demonstration.

Afterwards, the instructor had everyone pair up with somebody else and go through the same process, and interestingly, everybody experienced the same results. The instructor went on to explain that he was using this exercise to show us just how easy it is to move our center of power.

Shihan Adams had been talking about learning how to use our "center" in aikido class since the day I began my training. I had heard the phrase "stay centered" for years in other aspects of my life, with little more than a passing understanding of what it meant. However, this one demonstration brought home a much clearer picture not only of where our true physical center of power is (an inch-and-a-half or so below our belly button), but also how easy it is to engage or disengage ourselves from that center. Suddenly, staying centered meant something more to me than some pie-in-the-sky ideal that I may or may not ever be able to achieve in my lifetime.

With a better understanding of where to find my physical center and how to get and stay centered, my work in aikido began to blossom. Now don't get me wrong, I was, and still am, a long way from being good at aikido—after all, like horsemanship, aikido is a lifelong journey with no real end—but I did find that all of the techniques were easier to perform when I was centered. In fact (and no real surprise here), pretty much the only way aikido can work is if it's performed from the center.

Oh sure, like any martial art, the techniques in aikido can work to some degree when you're outside your center, but you end up engaging a tremendous number of muscles you don't really need to use. Using more muscle requires more adrenaline, and more adrenaline usually means the body isn't performing efficiently. In a time of real stress, if your body isn't performing efficiently, it fatigues very quickly. If you're engaged in a fight with a bigger opponent and your body wears out quickly, your opponent has a huge advantage.

When the art of aikido is performed properly, even the small or meek can defend themselves successfully against opponents of any size or strength. Of course, in order for the art to be performed properly, you must first be able to work almost exclusively from your center of power, not just from sheer muscle.

Once I began to get a handle on working from my center in aikido, I quickly began studying how working from my center could translate to my work with horses. What I found had a profound effect on the way I looked at my work, opening doors to things I had never thought possible.

When we ride a horse, we usually pay the most attention to the position of our hands, legs, and seat. We do this because we have been taught the importance of positioning in applying effective aids or cues to the horse, as well as in keeping proper balance in the saddle. Now, I'm certainly not going to argue with that way of thinking because I agree with it. There's no question that the placement of our hands, legs, and seat is always going to be critical to effectively communicating with the horses we ride.

However, over-reliance on hands, legs, and seat can lead to a mechanical feel from the horse. While the movements and responses coming from the horse may all be there, they may lack a smooth flow from one action to the next.

This happens with just about everyone I've ever watched ride, and it happens in my own riding. A rider cues the horse for, say, a transition from a walk to a lope using a light leg cue. The horse makes the transition, but just before the transition, there is often a very slight hesitation from the horse. It isn't very noticeable, but it's definitely there, kind of like the way an older car feels when you step on the gas. The car goes, but it's almost like it has to warm up to the idea first.

That little hesitation is something I first noticed many years ago, and as time went on and I saw it in more and more horses, no matter who was riding them, I just sort of dismissed it as the way things were. After all, we're talking about two separate individuals, a human and a horse, each with a great number of independent, moving parts in their bodies, and all of those parts have to get headed in the same direction at the same speed, once the cue for the movement is given. So I just figured it was natural for that little hesitation to be there. In order to eliminate it, many people use spurs or a riding crop to develop a more "responsive" reaction.

As I studied the proper use of the center of power in aikido, I began to look at that hesitation between horse and rider differently. When performing a technique in aikido with a partner, the goal is to have a flow of seamless energy from the time the person (*tori*) makes contact with his partner (*uke*), until the technique is completed. There should be no hesitations, no glitches, no stopping, and really not even any thought involved—just a smooth flow of energy from one spot to the next between two moving individuals.

Of course, in order for all that to work, it is imperative for the *tori* to be working from his or her center and not from the extremities. The extremities (arms and legs) are to be little more than extensions of the center and are simply used to *direct* the flow of energy, not to initiate it.

I began to wonder what would happen if I tried to ride my horse from my center. After all, riding is a lot like aikido. When we're riding, we really aren't initiating movement between the horse and ourselves. Rather, we are almost always directing or augmenting movement that is already there. That being the case, I felt riding would naturally be a great place to experiment with the idea.

It took me quite a while to find my center when I started aikido and much longer to use it effectively. I found there are a few things that need to happen before the act of centering can take place. The first, and perhaps most important, is establishing a quiet mind. That means developing the ability to shut out all distractions and concentrate only on the task at hand. It also includes looking at the task in a completely non-biased way, without preconceptions about whether it is right or wrong or good or bad.

Developing a quiet mind is not an easy thing to do, because we often give undue importance to relatively unimportant things in our lives. We have a tendency to get mentally overloaded with a lot of trivial thoughts that we really shouldn't spend any time on. A big key to helping me develop the effective use of my center was finding a way to prioritize what was going on in my life.

What I did was put everything that was going on in my life on a sort of "five-year plan." I took a good, hard look at each issue I was dealing with and asked myself if I thought it would be important to me in five years. If I thought it would be, I spent time on it, physically or mentally or both, until it was resolved. If I didn't think it would be important to me in five years, I simply refused to give it any attention whatsoever. I found I was much less encumbered mentally and therefore able to develop a quiet mind.

Once a quiet mind is established, the next step in effectively using your center is to work on breathing properly. In my case, a relatively deep, diaphragmatic breath that fills the entire lung and is exhaled in its entirety is what I found most beneficial. Breathing in this way allowed me to find any tight spots in my body that might hinder my ability to move freely and effectively. Finding and releasing these tight spots allowed me to establish what is known as "bottom weighting."

When bottom weighting occurs, it feels as if your entire body becomes unnaturally heavy and then somehow gets anchored right to the spot where you're standing. When this happens, it can become very difficult for someone to move you, no matter how much force is applied. That's what happened to the woman who helped with the centering demonstration at that clinic in Washington.

When all these aspects of centering come together, your physical power seems to increase and your movements in any direction have the potential to become extremely quick and efficient. I figured that if you could somehow bring this kind of feel and connection to riding, some pretty amazing things might happen between a horse and a rider. What the heck, it was worth a try.

My first venture into the world of riding from my center came on my horse, Smokey. Smokey has been a very busy horse all his life. His mind is always going about 100 miles an hour, and even though he was easy to start under saddle, he wasn't always an easy horse to ride due to his propensity for looking for things to do whenever he decided what we were doing needed a little spicing up.

I had been using Smokey pretty much exclusively for about a year after retiring my old horse, Buck, from the clinic circuit, and for the most part, things had been going along pretty well. There were just a couple of things I'd been trying to improve with him without much luck. I was looking for nicer stops and turns, as well as smoothing out his transitions. There was just a slight hesitation in each of these things that I was hoping to even out.

The first day I went to work on riding him from my center, we were at home in our arena. Nothing seemed much different while I saddled him or led him to the arena, but just before I got into the saddle, I took a second to center myself, just as I do on the mat in the dojo. As I mounted, I almost immediately felt a difference in Smokey. When I got on his back, he'd usually stand with relative indifference until I asked him to move forward. But this time, he sort of snapped to attention as soon as my backside was in the seat.

I gathered the reins and felt his energy come up underneath me like nothing I'd felt from him before. I asked him to move off, but instead of giving him my usual leg cue, I simply *thought* of moving myself forward from my center, just as I would if I were entering into an attack from my training partner. Much to my surprise, Smokey literally *shot* forward from a dead standstill right into one of the nicest lopes I'd ever gotten from him.

We had traveled about two laps around the arena in this magnificent canter when I decided to ask him to transition down, again using my center. I figured for the downward transition all I would need to do was just picture how it feels to finish a technique in the dojo, which I did. Smokey immediately hit the brakes like he was about to collide with a brick wall.

"Dang!" I thought to myself.

Well, a couple of things were obvious right off the bat. First, there was definitely something to the idea of riding from the center. I was getting responses from Smokey I'd never dreamed were possible. The second was, before I went any further with this idea, I'd better make a few adjustments.

For the next several months, Smokey and I experimented and then experimented some more, until finally I felt as though we had a fairly decent handle on what we were doing. We were eventually able to dial this kind of riding in to the point where our transitions were effortless, our turns were smooth and crisp, and our stops were soft and quick, all with little use of traditional cues from my legs, hands, or seat. On top of that, even the quality of his gaits greatly improved, and I wasn't even sure what I'd done to make that happen!

I kept working with the idea, and I began to realize that even though things seemed to be working really well using the concept of riding from the center, I was still missing a critical piece to the puzzle. You see, I had only been concentrating on *my* center. But when working with any partner, horse or human, there are two centers involved—that of the individual performing the technique and that of the individual receiving the technique.

The whole idea behind the art of aikido is to maintain your center, while encouraging the other person's center to go where you want it to go. That's also the key to successfully riding from the center—to somehow connect your center to the horse's center (which, as it turns out, just happens to be located almost directly under the rider) and then encourage the horse's center to go where you want it to go.

I went through a lot of trial and error, going back time and time again to restudy centering techniques learned from my aikido training, before finally stumbling on what I felt was a viable solution to the "connecting centers" dilemma. A simple suggestion Shihan Adams made in passing during an aikido class helped me find it. One night he mentioned the idea of visualization and how developing the ability to visualize a certain technique or movement can often be as powerful as practicing the technique itself.

Now, believe me, I know how weird this is going to sound, because not so long ago, if someone had told me the very thing I'm about to tell you, I would have thought they were nuts. But here it goes, anyway.

For several days I went around trying to come up with some kind of mental picture I could use to help me visualize connecting my center to my horse's center. The only thing I could think of was to picture my center directly over my horse's and visualize opening a small pathway between them, allowing them to connect. If I could do this successfully, I figured, I'd be able to direct my horse's center with mine, as we do in aikido.

I went back to Smokey and gave it a try. At first, it didn't make any difference. After about twenty minutes of riding, I decided to take a break from my experiment and just lope him around for a while. Smokey's lope was soft but relatively flat, even though he was using himself fairly well. There just wasn't much elasticity in his lope.

As we were going around, I recall the fleeting thought that one day I wanted to see if we could get him to reach underneath himself a little more and develop a nicer spring in his lope, when suddenly the movement he was offering changed. The speed of the lope didn't change, but without me consciously altering anything I was doing, he started reaching farther under himself with his hindquarters. Within three or four strides, I was getting movement like I'd never gotten from him before. His stride seemed huge, and the lift we were getting could have been that of a sixteen-hand warmblood, even though Smokey is only 14.3.

We made a couple of laps, just to make sure I wasn't imagining things, and then went back to the walk so I could think about what had just happened. It occurred to me that what was going on was a lot like what happens in martial arts. When we try to *make* something happen during a technique in aikido, whether we have our center engaged or not, generally the technique won't work or won't be optimally effective. However, when we just *let* it happen, the technique is not only successful, it is also very effective.

I believe that's what happened between Smokey and me. At first I couldn't get anything to work because I was trying to *make* it work. I was pushing on a closed door, a door that only opened in. The second I stopped pushing—trying to *force* the connection between the two of us—the door opened to me, and the connection was made. Then the information transferred, and the movement between us came through.

I know . . . it sounds too weird to be true. To be honest, if it hadn't actually happened to me, I'm not sure I would believe it either. But that doesn't change the fact that from that point forward, Smokey's lope was never the same again, and the communication between us has developed to a point where if I just think something, he often does it without any conscious cues on my part. Yup, it's weird all right. Definitely weird.

I continued to experiment with this type of riding with my other horses and also began sharing these ideas with a few of my students. About that same time, I visited with Shihan Adams about what I was finding using this idea of riding from the center, and he said he'd be interested in seeing what we were doing. I invited him down to the facility where our week-long clinics were held, some thirty miles away, to watch a couple of the riders I'd been working with use their centers to help their horses while jumping.

Shihan Adams showed up late in the day, after we had already put all the horses up, but Kathleen and Sharon, the two students I'd been working with on this concept, happily agreed to bring their horses back out. They each started out by doing some cue-less transitions, using only their centers to increase and decrease gaits or speeds within gaits. Then they went over a few of the jumps set up in the arena.

Sharon, who had also studied aikido, showed how she was able to dictate the height at which her horse would clear a jump by connecting her center to her horse's center.

"I'm going to raise my center and hold it for a second right over the top of the jump," she explained before making her run. "When I do, he should clear it with plenty of room to spare."

Sure enough, her horse cleared the jump by at least a foot-and-a-half.

"Now I'll do the same thing," she said, quietly bringing her horse to a stop near us, "but this time I won't raise my center quite as much. He'll still clear it, but he'll be closer to it when he does."

This time when they went around, her horse just barely missed the top rail of the jump. She went on to show how her horse would leave the ground in front of a jump or land after the jump differently, depending on how she used her center. The demonstration she gave was pretty remarkable, and I could tell by Shihan Adams' comments that he was pretty excited about the results we were getting with our work.

But then something happened that truly amazed all of us. While Sharon had been going over jumps, Kathleen had also been jumping her big gray horse and working on their transitions. They had turned at the far end and lined up on a diagonal jump near the middle of the arena. Their approach looked good, with nothing out of the ordinary going on, and I assumed they would glide over that jump, as they had all the others. But as they got right in front of the jump, Kathleen's horse suddenly stopped dead in his tracks, refusing to go over. In less time than it takes to blink an eye, Kathleen simply picked the 1,200-pound horse up with her center and floated him right up over the jump from a dead stop.

"Wow," she shouted in astonishment, as she cantered by. "Did you see that?"

"That was amazing," Shihan Adams nodded, with a hint of surprise in his voice. "I've never seen anything like *that* before."

"Me neither," I agreed.

Later I heard from members of our dojo that Shihan Adams had told the story of Kathleen's jump as an example of what can be accomplished when we connect with the power of our center. If the truth were known, I suppose I've told the story a time or two myself.

When it comes to horsemanship, and life in general, I'm finding there is no telling what kind of fun stuff we may discover if we take the time to open our minds a little and just go to looking.

Ever since I was a kid, working with horses has been one of the true joys in my life. As I got older, I couldn't believe someone would actually pay me to do something I would happily do for free. Then as time went on and I began doing clinics, the fun sort of went out of it for me. I began to take myself and my work too seriously, and eventually it got so bad, even riding became a chore.

I had allowed too many outside sources to influence me in a negative way, and I lost my center. Another way to say it is, for a while there, I lost both my physical and my mental focus on the things that are really important—that is, to keep my work simple and do it well, even if everything else went bad.

I can see now why staying centered is such an extremely important part of all our lives. At the same time, we shouldn't confuse being centered with being too intense. In fact, it seems to me that the more centered we become and the more knowledge we gain, the more we can allow ourselves simply to take things as they come. And that's when the simplicity of the work begins to reintroduce itself to us.

When we start into horsemanship, we all learn how to keep a leg on each side and our minds in the middle. Then, the more we learn about that one little premise, the more we begin to see how many layers there really are to it . . . the ultimate possibilities and the endless routes to new discoveries. We begin to see how the horse can actually become a vehicle to lead us away from the things that aren't important to us in our lives or lead us to the things that are.

In short, what we know about the horse and how well we are able to ride often become a symbol of our knowledge, power, control, and achievement.

As time goes by and we begin to understand how working with horses and riding them truly affect our lives, only then can we start to appreciate the simplicity of it all. What it really all boils down to is one simple idea . . . *keep a leg on each side and your mind in the middle.*

12

Circles

"Well," I asked my assistant, Kathleen, as we left the dojo following the aikido class she'd come to watch, "what did you think?"

"Man," she replied, with a hint of amazement in her voice, "I've never seen so many circles!" She hesitated, looking out the car window into the darkness. "Maybe I was just more aware of them because we've been talking about them lately. But . . . boy, it seemed like there were circles everywhere!"

"It's good if that's what you were seeing," I commented. "If people see circles in our work, then we know we're doing it right."

What Kathleen had seen at work in the class that night is one of the principles at the heart of aikido—circular movement. This type of movement is the foundation of nearly every aikido technique and is used to direct an opponent's energy to the most peaceful solution possible. Sometimes that means slowly and quietly diffusing the energy until there is simply none left; sometimes it means turning the opponent's energy against him in a way that brings it to a more abrupt stop.

As I mentioned, the word *aikido* translates to "the way of harmony," and the harmony aikido seeks to develop is the same kind found in nature itself. Even the circular movement that gives power and direction to the techniques is modeled after forces in nature.

After all, there are no more powerful forces in nature than those comprised of water or winds driven with circular movement—tornadoes, whirlpools, cyclones, typhoons, and hurricanes, for instance. In our dojo, hardly an aikido class goes by without someone describing a person performing a technique as being "in the eye of the hurricane" or "the calm in the storm."

It's pretty difficult to study an art like aikido and not notice the effects circular motion has when it's used properly on an opponent. It's so effective that even an almost imperceptible twist of the wrist at the appropriate time can easily send an attacker flying helplessly through the air.

For me, the study of circular movement became so important that it wasn't long into my training before I began seeing circles just about everywhere I went. In particular, I began seeing the importance of circles and circular movement when it comes to just about any kind of work we do with horses, no matter what activity or discipline we're talking about.

For instance, just look at one of the most popular tools used by trainers all over the world today—the *round* pen. The arena where horse shows take place is referred to as a show *ring*. Watch any horse show, whether dressage or reining or anything in between, and take note of how many circles or partial circles the horses are asked to perform. If a horse in a pleasure class is asked to reverse direction on the rail, you will almost always see the horse execute some form of circle. In a jumping class, the horse and rider make numerous turns and circles lining up for the jumps.

When someone asks his horse to do a one-rein stop or disengages the horse's hindquarters, he uses circular movement to achieve it. When a reiner does a spin . . . lots of circles there. Team ropers not only use a quarter-circle to turn the steer they catch, but they use countless circles when they spin their loops overhead before throwing them to catch the steers. Even the simple act of longeing a horse is performed in a *circle*.

I could go on, but I'm sure you get the point. We use a lot of circles in horsemanship. Sometimes those circles are beneficial, sometimes not.

❄

"See what I mean?" the woman on the big red gelding shouted as she flew by my horse, Buck, and me as we stood in the arena. "I just can't get him to slow down." Her voice faded somewhat as she blew past.

She reached the far end of the arena, grabbed her inside rein, and cranked the gelding's head around, forcing him into a small circle, effectively taking the use of his hindquarters away and grinding him down in what is known as a one-rein stop. She kept his head pulled over to her boot as the horse's feet danced nervously beneath him.

"This is the only way I can get him back to me," she told me. "But as soon as I let him go . . ."

She slowly allowed the gelding's head to straighten, and as if he were a train pulling out of the station, the gelding took a couple tentative steps, then a few faster ones, and finally he was off to the races again. He traveled about fifty feet back towards us at nearly a full-blown gallop and the woman pulled him around into another one-rein stop. The gelding once again danced nervously in place, the veins in his neck sticking out, his nostrils flared, and the whites of his eyes showing.

"Any suggestions?" she asked, with a hopeful smile.

"Is this pretty normal behavior for him?" I questioned.

"I'd say it's a little worse today, because we're in a new place and all." She looked down at the heavily breathing, quivering mass underneath her. "But yes, it's pretty normal. The kids that rode him before I bought him . . . all they did was saddle him up and make him run, so I think that's all he knows." The gelding tried to straighten himself out, but she kept his nose bent around to her boot.

"At first, letting him run like that was kind of fun. But now I'm a little tired of watching everything go by at a blur."

"How long have you been doing the one-rein stops to try to slow him down?"

"I don't know," she looked down at her now bit-chomping gelding. "Maybe five or six months. Before that I would just put him in a straight line and let him run 'til he got tired, but it takes a really long time for him to get tired."

"I see," I said, as Buck and I rode over to her. "Well, let's try something a little different with him then."

"Sounds good to me," she replied. "Anything's gotta be better than this."

I agreed that it appeared as though the gelding was running off because he thought it was what she wanted him to do. However, from the look on his face while he was running, he sure didn't seem to like having to run off. In fact, he really seemed pretty worried about the whole situation, and it seemed he'd be happy to try an alternative solution, if we offered him one.

Before moving on, I explained to the woman that I look at the kind of nervous energy her horse was offering up like it was water in a river as it flows downstream. As long as the water can move freely, within the confines of its banks, everything is okay. However, if someone places a dam in the river—and not a very well-built dam at that—problems begin to occur.

The previously free-flowing river comes up against the dam and outwardly appears to stop its movement. Yet the river continues to flow into the dam with the same amount of energy it would have if the dam weren't there at all. Before long, that energy wears at the poorly built dam until it breaks, and then we not only have a mess downstream, as the water floods, but we also have a mess upstream where the water had been held before the dam broke.

That's how I saw her horse's energy. The one-rein stop she was using was like that poorly built dam. It contained the progression of his energy for a time, but sooner or later that dam was going to break and we were going to have a mess on our hands.

"Let's try this," I suggested. "Instead of doing a one-rein stop when he tries to run off, let's try to allow him to continue to move his feet, but in a more productive way."

"Okay," she said, still holding the gelding's head to her boot. "How do I do that?"

"Let him go straight, but the second you feel him trying to break out of his walk or build up more energy than what you're looking for, immediately begin turning him in a circle, serpentine, or figure eight. In other words, allow him to keep moving, but don't allow him any straight lines when he does."

I explained that by turning him in a one-rein stop every time he ran off, we were telling him what we didn't want, but we weren't replacing the behavior with what we did want. As a result, we kept saying "no" to the only thing he knew how to do. Without anything else in his repertoire, he could only keep offering the same behavior over and over. Because we weren't giving him an alternative, he was frustrated and worried. We had to somehow show him the correct behavior without making him feel bad about what he was currently offering, and the way we would try to do that was through circular movement. We would use the circles, serpentines, and figure eights to diffuse and direct his energy without actually stopping it.

I went on to suggest she be mindful of the horse's behavior before and after she turned him. The key to her helping him slow down would not only be the timing of her turn when he started to speed up, but also the timing of her release when he offered to slow down. The second he offered to go faster, she needed to turn him. That way, she could address his "thought" of speeding up, theoretically making it easier for her to help him change that thought.

The second her horse offered to go the speed she wanted, she needed to let him go straight. By doing so, he would hopefully start connecting the act of going straight with the slower pace she wanted, and he could begin to learn a better, quieter way to go. I warned her that, to start with, he might only be able to take a couple of slow steps before he'd feel like he had to take off again. And if that was the case, it was okay. But as quickly as she could, she needed to put him right back into one of the turns until he began to slow down again.

After discussing the new plan, she decided to give it a try. She gradually let the gelding's head return to the straight position, and just like before, he started out by walking slowly forward. Within a few steps, it was easy to see his energy build and his pace pick up. The woman quickly, but softly, put him into a twenty-foot circle to the right, and as she turned him, the gelding tensed, and it appeared he was going to shoot into a trot, but he didn't. He made over a lap in the circle and then relaxed and drifted into a nice, soft walk. The woman immediately let him go straight.

He took about half a dozen quiet steps before his energy started to build. Just before he broke into a trot, she turned him in a circle, this time to the left. He looked as though he wanted to jump into a trot when she turned him, but he quickly settled down and went back to his quiet walk.

After about ten minutes of working with him in this way—sometimes doing circles, sometimes serpentines, sometimes figure eights—the woman and her horse were able to make about a quarter of a lap in a soft, quiet walk before he felt like he had to jump forward. Another ten minutes later, they were making about half a lap quietly. Thirty minutes later they could go all the way around the arena without the horse trying to move out of his walk. That was where we quit for the day.

The next day, when she got on and cued the gelding for his walk, he walked—first making one lap, then two, and then three, without any attempt to move out of it. In fact, there was no sign at all of the worried horse we'd seen the previous day . . . until we asked him to move from the nice walk he was in to a trot. Immediately, the worry—and the speed—returned. Without missing a beat, the woman quietly and softly put him into a turn. After three or four laps in that twenty-foot circle, the gelding's trot slowed considerably, and she let him go straight.

The horse was only able to travel a short distance before he felt he had to speed up, and again she turned him. This went on for only about forty minutes before she and her horse were traveling around the arena, lap after lap, in a nice, soft, slow jog. The horse's face and body were relaxed, and we could hear him breathing rhythmically as he quietly trotted past.

We repeated the entire process in the lope and had good results even more quickly. By the end of the four-day clinic, the woman and her horse could quietly walk, trot, or lope and regulate the speed of each gait without any trouble at all.

For me, this situation really brings home the power of circular motion when it's applied properly. In this case, using circles to help the horse diffuse and direct his energy was much more helpful than using circular motion to try to stop his energy. That's not to say the one-rein stops she was using previously were bad. It's just that in this horse's case, they weren't allowing the two of them to get to the root of the problem, and to some degree, they were even feeding into it.

"Well," I said to the lady, as she stood with her horse in the round pen, "what would you like to do today?"

"He's really a nice boy," she quickly replied. "Especially for a stallion. But for whatever reason, he really doesn't want me to put a bridle on him. I've had his teeth and ears checked; I have him looked at regularly by a chiropractor; and I spent two years finding a saddle that fits him, so I doubt the problem is physical or saddle fit. I've worked for hours teaching him to put his head down, which he does without any problem at all. It's just that when I go to put the bridle on, he refuses to let me."

"Okay," I said. "Why don't you go ahead and show us what he does when you try to bridle him?"

The woman went to the fence and picked up a very nice leather bridle and returned to her horse. He was standing in the middle of the pen, head down and nearly asleep. As she lifted the bridle into position, he ever so slowly turned his head to the right, away from her, and stepped forward into her with his left shoulder. She had to step out of his way or get run over, effectively stopping the bridling process.

"That's what he does?" I asked.

"That's it," she replied. "He does it every time, too."

"Let's try it again," I urged.

"Okay," she said, with a bit of resignation in her voice.

She slowly moved the bridle up toward his face, and again he turned his head to the right and stepped forward, pushing his left shoulder into her.

"What happens if you try from the other side?" I asked.

"He'll do the same thing, except he turns his head to the left instead of to the right."

"Can we see that?" I questioned.

"Sure," she said, stepping to the horse's right side and raising the headstall. As if on cue, the stallion slowly turned his head to the left this time and walked into her with his right shoulder.

"What happens if you try to straighten his head back toward you when he turns it like that?"

"Then he just starts fighting to get it turned back," she said. "And he's a whole lot stronger than I am."

"Okay," I said, as I entered the round pen. "Do you mind if I give it a try?"

"Be my guest." She handed me the headstall.

It was clear to me that the horse was offering a learned behavior, undoubtedly taught to him inadvertently by his owner. But I saw an opportunity to work on a solution by trying a couple of aikido principles I'd been studying, one being the act of *going with* and the other being the use of *circular motion*.

I took up a position on his left side, just as his owner had, and moved the bridle into position to put it on him. Just as he had with his owner, he slowly turned his head to the right and stepped forward into me. Instead of taking the bridle away and stepping away from him, as his owner had, I simply followed his head to the right with my hands and followed my hands with my body. In other words, I just took what he was already doing and augmented it. I *went with* the motion he was presenting, instead of trying to fight it or get out of his way.

His head swung effortlessly all the way to his shoulder and I helped him hold it there for only a couple of seconds before he suddenly shot backwards a couple steps in an effort to straighten his head. Once he was straight, he stood there with a surprised look on his face and his ears up, as if to say, "Hmm, that was different."

I went back, stood beside him, and moved the bridle up, and again he turned his head to the right. I stepped into his movement and helped him turn his head in the direction he'd chosen. This time he barely got his head to his shoulder before he shot backward to straighten his head.

I lined up for a third time on his left side, and this time he tried something different—he turned into me, to the left. I stepped slightly out of the way and brought his head all the way to the left. Again, as his head neared his shoulder, he shot backward in order to straighten out. Now, the interesting thing was that each time he backed up and tried to get straight, he was actually getting a release for doing the correct thing—standing straight.

He shook his head slightly as he looked at me, but stood quietly as I approached for another try. This time as I brought the bridle up, he turned his head ever so slightly to the right, stopped, and straightened. I slowly offered him the bit, and he opened his mouth like a perfect gentleman and allowed me to slide it in. We stood there for a little while, as he quietly mouthed the bit, before I took it off and tried again. Each time after that, whether I put his bridle on him or his owner did, the stallion stood with his head down and opened his mouth pretty much on his own, as we slipped the bridle over his head and put the bit in his mouth.

Here was a case where we were able to find a way to blend with the circular motion the horse was already presenting and augment it slightly to get him to rethink his behavior. It was just our luck that he discovered exactly what we were looking for quickly, which told us he wasn't married to the previous behavior, which he'd been taught inadvertently. It didn't matter much to him whether he did that behavior or something else. One was just as good as the other as far as he was concerned.

Moving *with* his circular motion, as he turned his head away, provided incentive for him to search for a different answer, without causing him undue stress or worry. Isn't that the goal of every horseperson when working with horses?

As I mentioned, it has become increasingly difficult for me to view any situation involving horses, or life in general, without seeing some form of circle in it. That became very evident to me a few years back, when I was working with a young woman and her horse at a clinic in California.

It was the second day of the clinic, and we'd been working on a couple of relatively easy tasks with good success. The only problem was that every time I tried to explain something to the woman, she interrupted me, often telling me why she thought she should do it another way, explaining how this trainer or that trainer told her to do it, or sometimes just saying things completely unrelated to what we were talking about.

"Do you mind if I ask you a question?" I asked, when she stopped talking.

"No, not at all."

"Why are you here?"

"What do you mean?" she questioned.

"I mean . . . why are you here at this clinic?"

"I want to learn how to work with my horse better." She seemed somewhat confused by the question.

"Is it easier for you to learn when you talk or when you listen?"

She sat for a moment, giving the question some serious thought.

"You know what," she nodded, "you're right. I have been talking a lot, haven't I? I do that sometimes when I get nervous. I really do mean to sit quietly and listen. It's just that sometimes I can't help myself. I'll try to do better."

"Okay," I smiled. "Let's give it another try."

She worked very well with her horse for the remainder of the clinic, and from that point forward, she kept her interrupting to a minimum (although it seemed difficult for her). As I reflected on the clinic at the end of the day, I realized something she said during our conversation really struck a chord with me. Her admission that she had been talking, even though she meant to sit and listen, got me to thinking about my own interactions with people. I began to wonder how many times, if I stopped to think about it, I'd find myself talking when I really should be listening. I wondered how much important information I was missing because I wasn't patient enough to listen to what others had to say.

The night after having the conversation with the woman, I sat down in my trailer and wrote on a scrap of paper: "Never talk when you mean to sit." I put the paper in my wallet. Every once in a while I'd pull the scrap of paper out and read the line, as a reminder to myself to try to listen more and talk less.

The more I looked at the note, the more I felt something was missing. There were times when I was listening to someone talk but I didn't agree with him, and if that were the case, perhaps I *would* need to say something or perhaps take a stand. As a result, I added another line to the scrap of paper. That line read: "Never sit when you mean to stand."

After a few weeks of reading those two lines, I slowly began adding other lines to the scrap of paper. Eventually I ended up with a little verse, if you will, that read:

Never talk when you mean to sit.
Never sit when you mean to stand.
Never stand when you mean to walk.
Never walk when you mean to push.
Never push when you mean to strike.
Never strike when you mean to push.
Never push when you mean to walk.
Never walk when you mean to stand.
Never stand when you mean to sit.
Never sit when you mean to talk.

Now, this verse started out with one line, meant as a reminder to myself to listen when others were talking. But as the verse grew, it became much more than that to me. The verse has come to symbolize not only how I want to be when I'm around people, but also how I want to be when I'm around horses, and on a bigger scale, how I want to be in my life.

Never stand when you mean to walk. The third line, for instance, is a reminder that not all battles are worth fighting. Learning how to prioritize the things that are truly important in the here and now continues to be one of the big struggles in my life. I've come to realize I only have so much energy to expend on things in any given day, and I can't fight for every cause. Some things I simply have to walk away from. Sometimes I have to physically walk away, and sometimes I have to mentally walk away.

Never walk when you mean to push. The next line helps me to remember not to walk away from every situation. There are times, whether working with people or horses, when "pushing" may be the proper thing to do. I have experienced this firsthand in my aikido class, when I was sure I wasn't ever going to get the new technique I'd just been shown. Still, my teachers gently pushed and prodded me along until the technique came through, and I felt much better about the situation. I'm sure walking away from me would have been a much easier thing for them to do, but helping me learn was more important to them than letting me struggle.

Never push when you mean to strike. The fifth line is one that a good number of folks seem to have trouble with, when I share my verse with them. For some reason, the word "strike" has a tendency to send horse folks screaming off into the woods. The most common comment I hear is, "I could never *strike* my horse." The next most common comment I hear is, "I could never *strike* anybody."

Well, first of all, a strike doesn't always have to be physical. It could just be acting quickly in a situation that warrants quick action. It could be simply saying the word *no,* in a way that leaves the person you're saying it to absolutely no doubt you mean NO. It could mean refinancing your home when the interest rates are at their lowest point in years. It could mean finally getting that divorce from an abusive spouse, asking someone out on a date for the first time, or taking that trip to Florida that you always wanted to take.

And yes, it can also mean a physical strike of some kind. For people who tell me they could never physically strike anybody, my question to them is usually, "If someone attacked you or someone in your family on the street, would you defend yourself or your loved one?" The answer I generally get is, "Well, yes I could strike someone then, but it would be in self-defense, so that's different."

I agree that would be different than just walking up behind someone and cold cocking them in the back of the head for no particular reason, but the fact remains that the person who just said they would never strike someone actually *could* strike someone if they had to. And therein lies the reality of the physical strike. There are times and places where a physical strike is not only appropriate, but may also be necessary. Granted, those times are few and far between, but they do exist, nonetheless. It is my opinion we shouldn't shy away from the idea of striking, whether it's a physical strike or one of the other examples I used, because one day it may be the only option. If you eliminate it from your toolbox, you could find yourself in big trouble on that day when it's the only tool that will work.

That line reminds me to keep that option open and not be afraid to use it, if and when the time and circumstance is appropriate. It's also the "high-water mark" of the first half of the verse, which starts with the idea of sitting and listening and culminates with the idea of using a strike.

Now look at the second half of the verse. Using all the same words used in the first five lines, but changing them around a little, the lines take on different meaning.

Never strike when you mean to push. The sixth line reminds me to use restraint in all my dealings, whether with horses or people. You see, an emotional mind doesn't think clearly. When emotion begins to govern our work, we should always step back for a moment and reevaluate the situation, whether we're overly excited, sad, happy, or angry. If we're too emotional, we may strike out when we shouldn't, causing more harm than good. By keeping a calm head, even when everything around us is falling apart, we should be able to judge when a push is needed but a strike isn't.

Never push when you mean to walk. The next line reminds me of the hard time I was having with my work and what it took to fix it. Even when everything was so obviously going wrong for me, both physically and mentally, I still kept pushing on what was surely a closed door. It was only when I walked away from it, leaving some of my old baggage behind, that things began to turn around for me. If that ever happens again, hopefully I'll know when to stop pushing and walk away a little sooner.

Never walk when you mean to stand. Line number eight reflects the fact that there will always be times when it might be easier to walk away from or around a situation, than it is to stop and make a stand. A friend of mine was in a relationship that had obviously run its course, and for years she found herself simply making do (or walking around the situation) to keep the relationship going, in hopes it would get better. One day she finally woke up and saw the relationship was no longer a positive influence in her life. She chose to stand up for herself and her own mental well-being. After a few final efforts to salvage the relationship, she decided the best thing for her was to bring it to an end. From that point forward, her life and her work began to grow and flourish like never before.

Never stand when you mean to sit. The next line pertains to our ability to listen to one another and is the thing I've learned the most from over the years. We often find ourselves so busy taking a stand on some issue near and dear to our hearts that we forget to sit and listen to what others have to say about the issue. I am just now starting to understand that the ability to listen is truly an art that must be developed and practiced. When someone talks, we can either hear what we want to hear or we can really listen to what they're saying and learn something beneficial. Regardless, we won't hear anything if we stand in front of them like a rock, with our ears closed and our arms folded across our chests.

Never sit when you mean to talk. Finally we come to the tenth line. For me, this line is a reminder that while it is always good to sit and listen to what is going on around us, we shouldn't forget to get involved in the process. We all have valid thoughts, views, and ideas worth sharing, and there will be times when those thoughts and ideas should come out. Like I said, listening to others is good, but sharing ideas in return is what ultimately shapes us and helps us grow.

During the week-long clinics we hold in the summer, it has become sort of a tradition for me to give the students some sort of homework at the end of each day. This homework is always optional and is usually designed to help the students think about how they can incorporate the qualities it takes to work with horses into the rest of their lives. The following morning, before we start to work with our horses, we sit around over coffee and discuss what everybody learned from the previous night's homework. These morning meetings usually turn into a pretty enlightening discussion on the subject of awareness.

At any rate, a couple of years ago I decided to use the "verse" as the homework for the week-long clinics to see what, if anything, the students would get out of it. At the end of the first day, I'd give the students the entire verse. I then gave them only two of the lines to think about at the end of each day, as their homework for the night. The results of these homework assignments were pretty interesting, to say the least.

By that time, I'd been thinking about the verse for quite a while and had obviously formed my own ideas of what it meant. I guess I just assumed most everyone would come to much the same conclusions I had. I soon found that while a number of folks would come up with similar thoughts, many people found completely different and extremely interesting meanings.

We did have a handful of people that summer who came in each day and said they just hadn't had time to look at the two lines we'd given them the night before. We had some who would wait until everybody had given their thoughts on the lines, and then when it came their turn, they'd simply say they agreed with what everybody else said. There were a few people who would say that before they could even think about dealing with the verse, they first had to fix it grammatically.

A couple of people spent their time analyzing my motivation for giving the verse as homework, rather than thinking about the lines themselves. A few people said they lost the paper the verse was written on, a few got angry with the verse, some felt intimidated by it, and a few felt really good when they read it.

One woman came in each day and expressed her frustration at trying to get something out of the lines. She said a number of times that it made her uncomfortable and she wished we would give her some different homework to work on. Finally, on the third day she came to the morning meeting and announced she just wasn't going to do the homework, as long as it involved the verse. Seeing as how the homework was voluntary in the first place, I told her it was fine if she'd rather not bother with it.

"Okay," she said. "Then I won't do it. It's too upsetting for me to have to worry about trying to get something out of it."

"No problem," I told her.

The next day, out of the blue, this same woman joined the discussion and came up with some of the most profound ideas we'd had from anybody at the clinics up to that point. When we finished discussing her ideas, she told us that once she quit fighting with herself about trying to understand the verse, suddenly all kinds of ideas popped into her head, which I found very interesting.

In all the ideas people shared about the verse, there were always two observations that just about everybody agreed on. Everyone felt the lines were speaking directly about the power of intent. Specifically, if you *mean* to do something, do it! No fooling around, no second guessing, no hemming and hawing. If you mean to sit and listen, sit and listen. If you mean to push, push. If you mean to walk away, walk away. But whatever it is you *mean* to do, make a decision and go with it.

The second observation that just about everybody agreed on was the circular form of the verse. It starts in one spot, takes us somewhere entirely different, and finally ends up where it started, ready to begin again. I thought that was strange, because when I put the lines together on that little scrap of paper, I didn't really pay attention to the order in which they fell. Only after I took a look at it in its completed form did I become aware of how it makes a big loop back onto itself. I hadn't written it that way by design, yet there it was . . . another circle.

In our society, we seem to like things in nice, even, straight lines. Straight lines are quick and to the point. They get us to where we want to be much faster than if we have to take a more circuitous route. Straight lines are great tools when we need to get somewhere quickly, no doubt. There is something secure about being on a straight line, and maybe that's why we like them so much. Heck, there are times when we're traveling a straight line that we can see all the way to where we're going, and that's something that can be very comforting when comfort is what we're seeking.

I, too, stay on straight lines whenever I can. For instance, when we're on the road going from one clinic to another, we always want to get there as quickly as possible. It saves wear and tear on the horses we're hauling, on the equipment we're hauling them with, and on ourselves. Those straight lines of the interstates are sure nice when we have a long way to go and a short time to get there. But every once in a while, when we get a chance to get off the interstate and take the scenic route, we realize that while the interstate is no doubt faster, we sure do miss a lot if it's the only road we travel.

We all have a tendency to seek out those straight, flat, easy paths to travel in our lives from time to time. There's nothing wrong with that. But the older I get, the more I begin to see there will always be something to be said for those circuitous routes in our lives, as well.

I used to worry a little when I found the straight path I was on starting to make a few twists and turns, particularly when it came to my work with horses. I always looked at those twists and turns as roadblocks—obstacles that were doing nothing more than slowing my progress and preventing me from reaching my goal. I now understand those twists and turns are there for a reason. They are there to help put some circles back into my straight lines, and I believe that tucked away somewhere in all those circles is where the understanding lies hidden. Although straight lines no doubt get us where we're going more quickly, it might just be those circuitous routes that help us gain our knowledge, strength, and power.

Of course, you'll really never know for sure unless every once in a while you're willing to get off the highway and take that weather-beaten, meandering, old dirt road over there . . . the one that's not on the map and seems to disappear just around the bend. Maybe it's a dead end, maybe it's a shortcut, maybe it's the long way around, but one thing is sure . . . you will learn something by taking it that you didn't know before.

13

Honoring Our Teachers and Our Places of Learning

I came out of the tool shed carrying fencing pliers, staples, and a twenty-foot piece of barbed wire coiled up in a loop, and made my way to the hay barn where the old man was inside counting bales.

"I'm going out to fix that broke fence," I shouted, as I popped my head in the door.

"All right," he said, without looking back at me. "Do good work."

Nearly any time the old man had me start a new project, whether it was fixing fence, oiling tack, saddling a colt, or cleaning water tanks, he sent me on my way with those same three words . . . *Do good work.*

In fact, I had heard him say that phrase so many times over the years that the words had finally lost their meaning for me. "Do good work" had become a lot like "see you later," "have a good time," or any number of other innocuous phrases we hear so often that we end up paying no attention to them.

Little did I know at the time just how important those three little words would become to me and how one day they would help me put my role as a student, and as a teacher, into clear perspective.

I could feel beads of sweat running slowly down the middle of my back as I stood by the gate of the round pen in the heat of a late

171

Kentucky morning. The day started off warm—eighty-five degrees by the time I got up at 6:00 A.M.—and it had gotten steadily warmer as the morning wore on. Don't get me wrong, I never really minded working in the heat; after all, it does sort of come with the territory. Heat is one thing, but that Kentucky humidity . . . now that's a different story. I overheard someone say it was ninety-eight degrees with humidity at about ninety-seven percent, and it wasn't even noon yet.

On one hand, we were lucky, because the round pen was inside a large, covered arena, so at least there was some shade. On the other hand, there wasn't much of a breeze, so even though we were in the shade, it was like being inside a shady oven.

This was my first-ever adventure into the world of horse "expos," and to be honest, I was already thinking it would probably be my last. There was something just a little unsettling about working with a horse in the middle of what seemed like a glorified shopping mall, with thousands of people milling about. But there I was anyway. You see, I had only been doing horsemanship clinics full-time for about eight months at the time, and the woman who was booking my clinics for me thought it would be good exposure to be a presenter at this particular expo. I was just a fella who was fresh off a ranch up in the mountains. For all I knew, working at these big, multi-million-dollar expos was just one of the things you did as a clinician.

Anyway, that's how I ended up standing there in the stifling heat, looking at a young mare that was flinging her head, stomping her feet, and kicking at her belly in a futile attempt to get rid of the thousands of black flies that had somehow found out she was the only horse in the whole place that didn't get a dose of fly spray. This was my third day of working with her, and my overall job was to get her started under saddle in the six hours (one-and-a-half hours per day) that was allotted to me over the four days of the expo.

I really felt sorry for the little mare. At three years old, she'd never been off her home place, and after spending six hours in her first trailer ride just to get there, she was thrust into this circus-like atmosphere and expected to be able to pay attention to what I was trying to teach her.

On the first day, we worked with her in a round pen inside the main building, where it was cooler. The only way to get her to the round pen was to walk her down about a 150-foot-long section of aisle, through crowds of people and between rows and rows of vendors, all set up and selling their wares. She made it unscathed, but just barely.

On her first day, it was clear she was on sensory overload, but even at that, she tried very hard to find a way to be okay with what we were doing. We did little more on that day than work on leading and longeing. In her state of mind, I felt that was about all she could handle. On the second day, we were able to progress to ground driving.

Now, before I go any further, I should note that there were a lot of clinicians at this expo, all starting colts. To my knowledge, every clinician but me not only had their colt saddled on the first day of their four-day demos, but for the most part, they were also up and riding them on that first day, as well. That was the first time I'd actually seen colts started so fast, and it kind of took me by surprise to see everybody moving along so quickly.

In contrast, I was just going along with this mare the way I'd always started my colts. I began with leading and longeing, followed by ground driving, then saddling, and then saddling and ground driving. Only then (providing the horse was okay with everything we were doing), would I get on for the first time. Sometimes I varied the order of these things or the speed, but not very often.

Due to the trouble this little horse was having just getting used to her surroundings, I saw no particular reason to hurry things along, and so I was content to take my time and make sure she understood what was going on before moving to the next thing. At any rate, by the end of the second day, the little mare was leading, longeing, and ground driving pretty well. At the end of our session, I mentioned to the crowd that I planned on saddling her in our next session, providing she was in a good enough place mentally to do so.

So there we were, on the third day of the demo. Instead of working in the relative coolness of the indoor round pen, we were standing in the outdoor round pen under that covered arena, in the oven-like heat, surrounded by upwards of 1,500 people who had come to see the colt be saddled for the first time.

"Did we get some fly spray on her?" I asked the owner, who had just turned the little mare loose in the pen.

"Actually," she said apologetically, "she's allergic to most fly sprays. We've been looking for some non-allergenic fly spray all morning, but nobody seems to have any here."

I watched in sympathy as the little mare tried in vain to rid herself of the relentless swarms of flies buzzing around her head, neck, legs, hindquarters, and back. As I stood there watching her, I flashed back to a similar situation many years before, when I was working with the old man.

We were getting ready to saddle a young horse for the first time. It was late in the afternoon, and the mosquitoes from the nearby irrigation ditch were coming out in earnest. The horse was being eaten alive and, as a result, was stomping, shaking his head, and whipping his tail around, just as the little mare in front of me was. But on that day, instead of going on with his original plan to saddle the colt for the first time, the old man simply had me put him away for the day.

"Why didn't we just go ahead and saddle him?" I remembered asking.

"Because," he replied simply, "tomorrow's another day."

At the time, I didn't understand his thinking. After all, we were there; the colt was there; why not just go ahead and get it done? But on this day, I understood. I could see that even if we successfully got a saddle on her without her blowing up (something I already had my doubts about, due to the flies), she was so distracted that the chances of her retaining anything were pretty slim. The bottom line for me on that day came down to one thought . . . tomorrow's another day.

"Our plan was to try to put a saddle on the little mare for the first time today," I said to the crowd over the microphone, "but it's not looking like that would be such a good idea, so we'll probably pass on that and do a couple other things to see if we can help her get a little more comfortable, physically as well as mentally."

Within seconds of that announcement, the place went from holding over 1,500 spectators to holding less than fifty. In fact, the arena cleared out so fast you would have thought someone yelled "fire." At any rate, I went on and worked with the mare using the saddle pad to brush flies off her neck, face, legs, and hindquarters, which pretty effectively desensitized her to the pad. She even felt so good about having the pad on her that later in the session I was able to up the ante a little and place the saddle on her back (without cinching it down). So, all in all, the session went really well, and I felt it put us in a great position to do the actual saddling the next day, when we would once again be indoors.

Now, one of the responsibilities of a presenter at this expo was to go to a large room each evening and do about an hour-and-a-half question-and-answer session for folks who happened to show up. On the first two evenings, perhaps thirty or forty people showed up. On this night, much to my surprise, the room was packed with a standing-room-only crowd.

"Good evening," I smiled, as I took my place at the podium. "Any questions?"

Immediately, a sea of hands rose, almost in unison.

"Yes," I said, pointing to a middle-aged man in a cowboy hat sitting in the third row.

"So," he said, as he slowly got to his feet, "I'm interested in knowing why you didn't want to saddle that filly today."

I could see nearly half the heads in the room nodding in agreement.

"Well," I started, "we only get one chance to make a first impression. With the trouble she was having with the flies today . . . she's allergic to fly spray and was getting eaten alive . . . I just didn't feel it would be the best day to put a saddle on her for the first time."

Several hands went up, but the man continued.

"So, what you're saying is, if your horse don't like flies, you shouldn't ride when flies are out?" There was sarcasm in his voice.

"No, sir," I replied. "That's not what I'm saying."

"Well then, what *are* you saying?"

"What I'm saying is, I didn't feel this was the best day to saddle her for the first time. Tomorrow's another day."

"Don't you think she should get used to wearing a saddle when flies are around?"

"Sure," I shrugged. "It just didn't need to be today."

The man took his seat, crossing his arms over his chest, and I pointed to a lady near the back, who had already risen to her feet when she raised her hand.

"I was just wondering," she started, with a tone that sounded more like a statement than a question, "why is it you've been working with her for three days now, and you still haven't saddled her? It seems like you take a whole lot of time to do something most trainers do pretty quickly."

"I didn't know I was in a race," I smiled. She didn't. I stopped smiling. "It's just how I start my colts. It's how I was taught. Someone else might do it differently."

The rest of the night went on pretty much the same way. There were some folks who said they really appreciated the fact that I *didn't* saddle the mare, but overall it was a pretty tough crowd.

The next day we got the little mare saddled without incident, and she even offered to accept a rider when I started standing in the stirrup. Due to time constraints, I didn't actually get on the mare's back, something the owner said she felt confident in doing once she got home. I left the expo feeling pretty good about the work I'd done . . . but I haven't participated in another one of any kind since.

At first, I wasn't sure how to handle all the negative feedback I received about not saddling the mare on that third day. Some days when I thought about it, it wouldn't bother me at all; other days I'd be a little upset over it. As time went on and I began to see the futility of rehashing the matter, I quit thinking about it altogether, but I never really settled the matter in my own mind.

Something happened about seven years later that not only brought the entire incident back to the forefront for me, but also gave me a completely different perspective on the issue, one I'd never even considered before. It all came about when I attended my first aikido seminar, which was taught by So-Shihan Scott, Shihan Adams' teacher, who had traveled down from his dojo in Alaska to perform the seminar.

After only a short time at the seminar, I realized that So-Shihan Scott's style of aikido was a little different from my teacher's style. Yet even though there were obvious differences in styles of teaching and styles of aikido, for that matter, it was also clear the fundamental principles of the art itself were the same. Even though Shihan Adams had put his own mark on the way he practiced and taught aikido, he did not stray at all from the heart of what he had learned from So-Shihan Scott.

Although Shihan Adams had been away from So-Shihan Scott's dojo for a number of years and now had his own students and his own dojo, he was continuing to honor his teacher by staying true to the integrity of his teacher's work—work that had already been passed down for generations. In a sense, it didn't really matter if So-Shihan Scott or Shihan Adams was teaching, the heart of the work, the foundation, remained intact. So-Shihan Scott teaches with integrity, Shihan Adams learned with integrity, and now it is that integrity in the work that is being passed on to me and the other students in the dojo.

That's when I began thinking about the work I did at the horse expo. I realized I'd been bothered by the negative feedback about the way I worked with the mare. I felt it had been a personal attack on me and my abilities as a horse person. Looking back, that was certainly a very egotistical way of looking at it . . . as if I really mattered. Heck, what I was doing that day, or any other day for that matter, wasn't about me anyway, it was about the horse—and about the work itself.

Maybe what I was getting from folks during that question-and-answer session were personal attacks, and maybe they weren't. In the end it doesn't matter. What does matter is whether the work was effective and honored the spirit in which it was taught to me. Did it bring integrity and dignity to the horse? The only one that could really answer that question was the little mare I worked with, not the people sitting in the stands watching.

When it comes to my work with that horse, I can look back and see that my teacher taught with integrity all those years ago. In his own way, he showed me the things that were important to him and, ultimately, what he felt was important to the horse. He drove home certain points over and over, sometimes in a quiet way, sometimes a little louder, and sometimes in a way so subtle that I still haven't figured them out. But he never relented, and he never took shortcuts.

Now, for better or worse, I find myself the teacher, and it is my responsibility to bring those same qualities to my work that my teacher brought to his. As the teacher, I find it increasingly more important (especially the older I get) that the integrity of the work comes through for my students and comes back from my students. That means I need to teach with integrity, and they must try to learn with integrity. In other words, we both need to become more than just students of technique.

Now, please don't misunderstand me here. Proper technique in any endeavor is extremely important, and I'm not suggesting we take the understanding of technique lightly. It's just that technique is almost never the end-all to anything we do. You see, just as in martial arts, if we are just a student of technique, we will only be able to go as far as the technique can take us. But if we become a student of the art— or, in this case, the horse—the places we can go are boundless.

Interestingly enough, discovering this concept of honoring my teachers through the integrity of my work began to shed light on a couple of other issues I'd been struggling with for a while.

For about a year-and-a-half after I began my martial arts training, I walked through the front door of the dojo just like I walked through every other door. I'd turn the knob, open the door, and walk through, allowing the heavy spring on the door to close it behind me.

I always tried to walk through that door a good fifteen minutes prior to the beginning of class, and usually by the time I showed up,

Sensei Marty was already there, stretching and warming up. As a result, I never got a chance to see how he walked through the dojo door, not that I thought it was any different than the way I did.

One day Sensei Marty was running late, and I happened to get to the dojo before him. For the first time, I had the opportunity to see him walk in the door. I'd have to say, he came in much differently than I did. As quietly as possible, he slowly pulled the door open, paused briefly at the threshold, and then bowed respectfully before entering. He stopped again just inside the door and allowed it to swing softly into his backside. Then he inched himself forward so the door didn't make any undue noise as he entered.

Over the next several months, I arrived at the dojo before Sensei Marty on a number of occasions, and each time, I noticed he entered exactly the same way. Now, he had seen me enter the dojo many times in my nonchalant manner, and he never said anything about it. In fact, nobody had ever told me how to enter the dojo at all. Of course, it had been explained to me how to enter the floor area where we worked—stop before getting to the area, bow at the waist, and then enter—but there was never any mention of how to come through the front door.

Well, I finally figured that if Sensei Marty was entering the dojo the way he did, there must be a reason. So one day I just decided to follow his example, and I have ever since. I've come to understand that the act of bowing when entering the front door of the dojo, as well as at the dojo floor, is showing respect to the place where we come to learn and practice our art. Traditionally, the dojo is a place that is held in very high regard, as it gives martial artists a safe space to come and train, a place where we can concentrate only on our art and, for a time, be sheltered from outside distractions.

There is one other very important thing I learned from Sensei Marty about entering the dojo. It was something I noticed him doing but never gave much thought to. It was the foot with which he entered. I noticed early on that he always entered the dojo floor on his left foot. Prior to the beginning of one of the Thursday morning classes he teaches, without anyone asking, he explained his reason for entering the dojo on his left foot.

It goes back to the days when warriors carried swords. Because the sword was carried on the left hip, it was more difficult to draw the sword if the left foot was forward. Therefore, when someone entered a room using his left foot, he was showing the occupants of the room that he was coming in peace and meant no harm.

I suppose, about now, some folks might say, "Okay, so now I know how to enter a dojo, should I ever decide to do so. But what does this have to do with horsemanship?"

For me, it has many correlations, starting with the idea of showing respect for our place of learning. In the dojo there are certain, often unspoken, rules concerning one's behavior, whether you're a student or a visitor. As a student, you're expected to bow whenever entering or leaving the floor. You're expected to treat your teacher, as well as your fellow students, with respect and dignity.

When the teacher speaks, you are expected to sit quietly and listen, until he or she has finished speaking. Idle chatter should be kept to an absolute minimum, even though in most aikido dojos, there is almost always a certain "light air," if you will, that goes along with the training. It's not unusual to see people doing spectacular throws and falls and then smiling or even laughing right afterward. This comes from the positive feeling both parties get when the throw and fall are performed properly. Even with that, when you're in class, you're there to train, not talk. There will be plenty of time to talk when class is over.

As a visitor to a dojo, you are also expected to show respect to the teacher and students in class by sitting quietly, especially when the teacher is speaking. Loud talking of any kind, particularly any negative comments toward the students or teacher, is considered extremely rude behavior and is not tolerated. Again, the dojo is supposed to be a safe place for students to come and train, a place where they can concentrate on their art without having to worry about outside distractions. If a visitor to a dojo has, in some way, become a distraction to the students, that person may be asked to leave.

It all boils down to common courtesy. It's about honoring the place of learning, as well as honoring the people inside. Pretty simple concept, really. At least in the dojo, it's a simple concept. When it comes to finding that same courtesy in other areas of life . . . well, that's often a different story.

When I began doing clinics, for instance, I was quite surprised at the rudeness some folks displayed when they were auditing and sometimes even when they were riding in the clinic. There were times when a rider or spectator would ask me a question, and as I began answering, he would interrupt or sometimes just talk right over the top of me without even letting me get an answer out.

There were other times when I'd be explaining something or answering a question, and I'd have to stop and wait until the boisterous conversations of people in the audience died down. Often those conversations were so loud they overpowered the P.A. system, which isn't an easy task, considering I was using a ten-inch, 150-watt, amplified speaker. What made some of those conversations even worse was they were full of negative criticism aimed at the rider in the arena.

One time I was working with a woman at a clinic who was a relatively new rider. It was the third day of the clinic, and we were working on some of the basics with her and her horse. The riding instructor she'd been taking lessons from was in the audience. While the woman and I were working in the arena, the instructor suddenly started yelling commands to the lady from her seat in the bleachers!

"Sit up! Heels down! Eyes forward!" came the voice from the bleachers.

I let the first three or four commands slide, thinking the instructor was just having a hard time controlling herself, but more came.

"Shorten your reins! Heels down! Eyes up!"

"Thanks for the help," I said over the mic, finally feeling as though I needed to say something, "but today she's my student."

"Well, excuse me," came the forced apology.

For the first several years I was doing clinics, I often tried to let rudeness from riders or auditors slide, figuring it was just the way it was. But I must say, over time, that type of behavior really started to eat away at me. Now, don't get me wrong here. Not everyone who attends clinics is rude. In fact, the majority of folks are just the opposite, very respectful of the venue and cordial to the folks riding in the clinic. But when folks who are rude show up, they sure stick out.

I finally realized the reason some folks were rude at the clinics was because I was allowing it. In the dojo, proper etiquette is expected from students and guests alike, so that training can proceed in the most productive and beneficial manner. I had to ask myself, if certain expectations for behavior worked in the dojo, why wouldn't they work in a clinic? After all, shouldn't an arena or round pen also be a dojo . . . a safe place for students, whether horses or humans, to work on their art? Well, the answer to that is simple—of course it should.

When I began the 2002 clinic season, I decided to treat each venue as my dojo. When I looked at the venue as my dojo, I suddenly became much more aware of my responsibility to protect it and the people who entered, especially the riders. Prior to beginning each clinic, I found myself standing in front of the spectators, welcoming them and explaining my expectations for them.

"What I would like all of you to do," I would say, "is treat the folks riding in this clinic—the people who have brought their horses for you to watch and learn from—treat them the way you would like to be treated if you were out here riding. Give them some support and treat them with the dignity and respect they deserve. I also ask that you please refrain from any negative comments about the riders today when you're visiting amongst yourselves during the sessions. If you find you absolutely have to say something negative about a certain horse or rider, please go somewhere else to say it."

I immediately saw a difference in the behavior of auditors and riders when I gave this little speech. People were much more supportive of each other, and the rude talk that had been so prevalent in the past just seemed to disappear. Oh sure, there was the occasional comment now and again, but for the most part, the atmosphere at the clinics genuinely changed for the better.

Eventually, I made the decision not only to treat every venue as a dojo, but to enter each one as if it were a dojo as well. Every time I walked through a gate, I did so by stepping through with my left foot first.

I began performing this gesture as an afterthought one day when a young, rambunctious gelding was brought into the round pen where I was standing and turned loose. The youngster was worried about his buddy back at the barn and began running frantically along the rail. On his second lap, he nearly ran me over, as I made my way to the gate to pick up a halter and lead rope hanging there. At first, I felt a twinge of aggravation, but almost without thinking, I simply went to the gate and stepped out, closing it behind me. I stood there for a couple of seconds before picking up the halter, opening the gate, and very deliberately stepping back in, this time entering with my left foot. My aggravation immediately disappeared, and I was ready to go to work with a different attitude.

That one simple act had such a profound effect on me that I just adopted it as part of my everyday routine. It's especially important to me when I'm working with overly troubled horses (or riders and spectators, for that matter). Just as when I enter the dojo back home, I use it as a small reminder to myself that I come to the arena in peace and I mean no harm. The simple act of entering the arena on my left foot gives me that little extra incentive to stay focused in my work, to not feed into any unwanted behavior a horse is offering up, and to not get involved in any undue confrontations people might be "offering up."

As I said earlier, the older I get, the more important the integrity of the work I do has become. Integrity in my work has always been important, but now I can see more clearly how the work I do today is a direct reflection on what my teachers, both horse and human, have passed along to me.

That's why the old man used to tell me to do good work. It's because the work I do today is a legacy of the work he did back then. The work that my students do is also part of that legacy. Because of that, I realize I not only owe my current students my very best effort every time I step into a pen with them, but I also owe my teachers my very best effort, as well. Only then can the spirit of their work be passed along in the way in which they intended.

These days, I see my occupation as one of working with horses. But my job is to honor the spirit of the work I do, as it was once taught to me, in much the same way Shihan Adams honors the spirit of what So-Shihan Scott taught him. Maybe the style of the work has changed a little over the years, as it should, but the foundation is, and always will be, the same.

To me, that means I need to be a student of the horse, not just a student of technique, and I should try to do my work with honor, integrity, and dignity. Sometimes that means not saddling a colt for the first time when she's being eaten alive by flies. Other times it might mean protecting a student from the harsh words of spectators.

It's not always an easy path to follow. Admittedly, sometimes I get it right, sometimes I don't. But I do believe that somewhere in the effort is where the honor to my teachers, and to my places of learning, resides.

14

The Price of the Ticket

It had been three years since I'd retired my old horse, Buck, and for the most part, he seemed to be getting along with the idea pretty well. I must admit though, I'm not so sure either one of us liked the change at first. Rightfully so, I guess. Buck and I had been through a lot together in the seventeen years we were partners.

Once, when one of the hands on the ranch accidentally left a gate open, it was Buck and I who went out in the middle of a moonless night and brought the herd back safe and sound. We had worked hundreds upon hundreds of cattle and horses, ridden thousands of miles of trails together, been on numerous search and rescues in the high country of the Rocky Mountains, and had even been in a few parades.

In his time, Buck carried everyone from movie stars and professional athletes to folks who were physically handicapped, as well as plenty of everyday folks who just wanted to learn how to ride. The local rodeo queen used Buck when her horse became injured, a twelve-year-old boy rode him in a western pleasure class, and he was the first horse all three of my kids rode by themselves.

When I began doing clinics, Buck effortlessly switched gears and went from a working ranch horse to a working clinic horse. Together, the two of us crisscrossed the country more times than either one of us probably cared to recall, and in all that time, he never faltered, never quit, and never let me down. He saved my bacon on at least half a dozen occasions that I can recall (usually when I'd gotten us into a spot we shouldn't have been in, in the first place), and in fact, my saddle still holds the teeth marks of a young horse that came after me but missed because Buck moved me out of the way just at the right time.

As you can imagine, I would have ridden Buck forever, if I could have. But unfortunately for me, time and age ultimately began to catch up with him. It always had been notoriously hard to keep weight on Buck, but by the time he reached his late teens, his weight became even more of a concern. Our clinic and travel schedule was pretty grueling, and finding a feed supplement on the road that worked well for him was not easy. On top of that, he also developed an intermittent lameness problem in his front end that kept vets, chiropractors, farriers, and me guessing for the better part of two years.

We eventually got his lameness issue sorted out, and I found a feed supplement that actually kept weight on him. By that time he was in his early twenties, and it had become clear he had reached the end of his ability to sustain any kind of regular work schedule. So, as much as I hated to do it, in November of 2000, I regretfully retired him.

Even though he was retired, he didn't quit working all together. My son, Aaron, rode him quite a bit during the summer months, and I even let a student use him for a couple of days' worth of work at one of our week-long clinics in 2003. And I gotta tell you . . . the way Buck worked with that woman in the clinic was definitely in typical "Buck" style.

On each morning of the week-long clinics, the students and I get together to discuss what our plans are for the day. Gail's horse had come up lame the day before, and Buck was the only other horse we had available to fill in. As a result, Gail had ridden Buck for a couple of hours the day before and would be riding him all day that day.

"What are you and Buck going to do today?" I asked Gail.

"Well," she smiled, "I noticed yesterday when I took Buck up to a gate, he didn't really know how to get me up to it so I could open it. So, one of the first things I want to do today is teach him how to open gates."

I was grinning inside. I'd probably opened and closed somewhere in the neighborhood of 10,000 gates from Buck's back in our time together.

"That should be . . . fun." I couldn't help but smile.

I don't know if it was fun for Gail or not, but it sure was fun to watch. She took Buck to the arena gate, and for the next hour or so, Buck patiently went exactly wherever she asked him to go. The only problem was, where she *thought* she was asking him to go was not anywhere near where she was *actually* asking him to go. Every time she thought she was cueing him to go sideways, she was actually cueing him to go forward. When she asked him to go back, she was actually asking him to go sideways. When she asked him to go forward, she was cueing him for a turn on the haunches, and so on.

Buck worked for her with the patience of a saint, and eventually, they got in position to get the gate open and go through. Once on the other side of the gate, they were another half-hour or so getting it closed again. When they did, Gail praised Buck like he had just won the Triple Crown, which I'm sure he appreciated.

Later in the afternoon, Gail decided she would work on Buck's second gate lesson. But this time, things went a little differently. Gail rode Buck toward the gate, and as soon as he saw where they were going, he just pretty much took over. As they neared the gate, Buck did a perfect turn on the forehand, which he then turned into the prettiest little side pass you'd ever care to see. He stopped next to the gate and put Gail in the perfect position to open the gate latch.

Gail reached down and opened the latch, and as soon as she did, Buck took one step back so he could reach the gate with his nose, turned his head into the gate, and gave it a soft shove. Then, without Gail having to cue him, he turned and walked through the open gate, swung his back end around so he was once again parallel with the gate, nudged the gate closed with his nose, and then stood there waiting for her to latch it, as if he were saying, "You're going to have to do this part; I don't have opposable thumbs."

Later that day, Gail would tell me if she hadn't been on him when he did all that, she wouldn't have believed it.

"Believe me," I chuckled, "I know just what you mean."

❀

Aaron rode Buck a few more times that summer and into the fall, but for the most part, Buck slowly slipped back into retirement mode, which consisted mostly of standing under shade trees and eating anything that was put in front of him. It was clear he had become the patriarch of our small herd of seven head, and he appeared content with his role as the elder statesman.

Since I retired Buck, I had been using Smokey, a young gelding we had raised, pretty much full time as my clinic horse, and he had been working out really well overall. The only problem with Smokey was his size. At just under 14.3 hands and maybe 1,000 pounds soaking wet, he was a little small for some of the work I was asking him to do in the clinics. This became evident one day during a week-long clinic.

One horse at the clinic was afraid of water and refused to even attempt to put his feet in a small water crossing we had on the place. The owner worked with him off and on for a few days without much success. The horse was pretty happy to approach the crossing, which was about fifteen-feet wide and went from just a few inches deep near the banks to almost belly-deep in the middle, but he absolutely refused to put even his toe near the water itself.

The owner had abandoned trying to ride the 15.1-hand, 1,200-pound gelding through the water the day before. He was working on trying to lead him through or, at the very least, just get him interested in putting a foot partially in the water, when he asked if I could help. The horse had pretty much decided he wasn't even going to try, and so he was standing very quietly and contentedly next to the crossing, half asleep, when I rode up on Smokey.

"You mind if I take his lead rope?" I asked the owner.

"Not at all," the owner replied. "Maybe you'll have more luck than I've had. He's pretty stuck."

I took the lead rope and slowly rode down into the crossing until Smokey and I were near the middle, where the water was the deepest. I took up the slack, made a little contact with the gelding, and waited to see what kind of a reaction we would get. At first, he just stretched his neck out without moving his feet, but after standing a few minutes in that uncomfortable position, he finally started to offer some sideways movement. It wasn't the direction I wanted, but at least it was movement, so I immediately released the pressure on the rope. He immediately stopped moving.

We continued along in just this manner for the next fifteen minutes or so, until he finally took a step forward, toward the water. When he did, I not only released the pressure, I rode out of the water and led him completely away from it for a minute. Then I took him back and started all over again. This time, he took some forward steps a whole lot quicker, which prompted me to ride out of the water again and take him away from it for a while. About twenty minutes later, he was standing next to the water, nose down, trying desperately to put his toe in it, which he eventually did. Again, I took him away from the water crossing for a minute or so before bringing him back.

This time, while Smokey and I were standing belly-deep in the middle of the crossing and encouraging the gelding to inch forward with the lead rope, he suddenly did something none of us expected. Without warning, the gelding stepped up to the water's edge, smelled it, took a little drink, then stepped right in, first with his left front foot, then his right. He seemed perfectly content, so I let him stand for a few seconds to get used to the idea and was just getting ready to lead him away when I saw his hindquarters begin to drop slightly.

"Uh-oh," I said to myself.

By dropping his hindquarters, the gelding was showing us he planned to come all the way into the water, which I didn't want him to do for a couple of reasons. The first was that I was hoping to introduce him to the water slowly, so I could just get him used to the *idea* of crossing. I didn't necessarily want the *act* of crossing yet. The second thing was that the water in the middle, where Smokey and I were, was deep enough that it might worry him unnecessarily.

What came next happened so fast that neither Smokey nor I had much time to react.

The gelding suddenly lunged headfirst into the water, landing with a huge splash right beside us. Without thinking, I took a quick dally around the saddle horn, as the gelding scrambled, jumped, and thrust himself up the opposite bank, effectively dragging Smokey and me with him.

Well, we all got a little wet in the water-crossing extravaganza, and once we were all safely up on the opposite bank, Smokey kept looking at the gelding as if to say, "What the heck's wrong with you? It's just water, for crying out loud!"

We all went back to work after a few minutes and were successful in helping the gelding feel better about crossing water. But the ease with which that gelding jerked us out of the water made me realize that Smokey just wasn't big enough to be able to do some things a horse Buck's size could handle with little effort. But since Buck was retired and I didn't want to put Smokey in that kind of situation ever again, I soon began looking for another horse I could use for clinics, one that was bigger and that would hopefully have the right temperament to spend weeks at a time on the road.

I had seen him only twice before, once when a friend used him to work some cattle and another time when he was standing in a pasture. He was a seventeen-year-old, ranch-broke gelding that, by all accounts, had been through a pretty rough life. He was about 15.1 hands and around 1,200 pounds, just the size of horse I was looking for, but he was a little jumpy and pretty protective of himself. Still, there was just something about him I liked from the very first time I laid eyes on him, and when my friend decided to put him up for sale, I went ahead and bought him.

On my way home from some clinics I'd done north of L.A., I swung in and picked up Mouse (a name he undoubtedly received due to his mouse-like color) from my friends, Shawn and Beth Anne, at their place near San Diego. I only had the chance to work with him a few times at home before I loaded him in the trailer and hauled him to Texas for a pair of clinics down there. I quickly found while Mouse did, indeed, have some issues, he was about as honest as the day is long and had as much "try" in him as any horse I'd ever had the privilege to ride. For the first time since I retired Buck, I felt as though I had another horse under me that I could count on if the chips were down.

After returning from our trip to Texas, I turned Mouse in with Buck, Smokey, and my little mare, Dancer, over at our barn, which is on the other side of town. That doesn't really mean much, because our town is so small, every part of it is only about five minutes away from any other part.

The barn has four stalls, and there's a 100' x 100' arena that we mostly use as a turnout. It was in this turnout where the four horses all ran together. While Dancer and Smokey all but ignored the new horse, I was pleasantly surprised to see that a bond developed almost immediately between Buck and Mouse. Within a day or so, the two of them were nearly inseparable. I even caught the two of them running and playing a couple times, something Buck hadn't done much of in the past few years.

A few weeks passed, and along about mid-December, it came time to take the horses down to their eighty-acre winter pasture. I loaded Smokey, Dancer, and Mouse in the trailer, but Buck had lost so many teeth in the past few years that he didn't do well trying to graze, and I was forced to leave him behind at the barn. It wasn't the first time Buck had been left alone. In fact, he had spent a great deal of time by himself over the years, including the previous two winters he'd spent at the barn while the other horses were out on pasture. Being left by himself didn't seem to bother him this time either, and I didn't see any change at all in his behavior—not until about ten days later, that is.

About a week or so before Christmas, I noticed a difference in the way Buck was acting. For years he had made a habit of meeting me at the gate whenever I went into his pen and would follow me around while I was cleaning up manure or filling his water tank. If I called his name, usually he would stop whatever he was doing, look in my direction, and nicker back. But suddenly that all stopped.

At least he was still eating well, and I took some consolation in that. But after a few more days passed, I noticed he was leaving some of the pellets I'd given him at his previous feeding. They were a complete-feed pellet that had become his mainstay, because when he ate hay, it usually just balled up in his mouth and fell out on the ground in little green wads.

He was eating enough to sustain his weight but not much more, and a few days before New Year's Eve, I mentioned to my wife I was concerned about him.

"I'm afraid one of these days I'm going to go to the barn and see he just lay down and died on me," I told her, as we drove into town one morning.

"I don't know," she said. "He looks better now than he has in years, and he's still eating good."

She was right. Even though he wasn't eating as much as he had a month or so earlier, he was still eating well. And the fact that he wasn't meeting me at the gate or answering me when I called could have been anything. Maybe it was the fact that the weather had gotten colder and wetter, and he didn't like having to spend a few days in the barn. Maybe he missed his friends or being out on pasture. Or maybe he was just getting old and cranky . . . it didn't seem likely, but who knows.

On New Year's Eve day, all that seemed to change. I was going to be performing with the band that night at our annual New Year's Eve gig, and I needed to be at the place about 4:00 P.M. to help set up equipment. As a result, I went to the barn to feed a little earlier than usual. Much to my surprise, Buck, who'd been standing off in the corner of the arena where he usually slept, came trotting over and met me at the gate. He followed me around, just like always, as I put his pellets and hay in his feeder and then went over to check the water tank.

For the first time in weeks, he seemed like his old self, and before I left, I stood and petted him on his head for a few minutes. The weather had broken a few days before. It had gone from cold and wet to unseasonably warm and sunny, and it was supposed to stay that way for the next several days. I thankfully chocked up Buck's dramatic turn in behavior to the change in weather and didn't really think all that much more about it, other than I was glad to have the old Buck back.

I knew I would be late for setting up, but I stayed and hung out with Buck for just a few more minutes before finally going back to the truck. Buck stood by the fence and watched, as I drove away.

Our gig went really well that night, the only drawback being that Wendy and I didn't get home until nearly 2:30 A.M. I'd hoped to sleep in the next day but could only manage to stay in bed until just after seven. I got up, had breakfast, and loafed around the house for another hour or so before deciding to head over to the barn to feed. It was weird though, because on the way over, I suddenly had this little knot in my stomach. For the life of me, I couldn't figure out why. As I got closer to the barn, the knot seemed to intensify, and as I pulled up into the driveway, I knew why it was there.

Over in Buck's favorite corner—the one where he always slept—lay his lifeless body. My heart sank as I sat staring at him from the seat of my truck.

Maybe he's just sleeping, I heard something in the far reaches of my mind say.

But I've been around horses long enough to know that just wasn't the case. I got out of the truck and went into the arena, glancing at his feeder as I passed it.

He finished his feed, I thought to myself.

I slowly made my way over to him. The practical side of being a horseman was already taking over. I stood over him and scanned the immediate area.

No sign of struggle, I thought. *Probably not colic. There would have been some sign of struggle for sure, and he probably wouldn't have finished his feed. Besides, Buck's never been sick a day in his life. Looks like he just lay down and went to sleep.*

I reached down and gently took hold of his front leg, checking for stiffness.

Still some movement in the joints, I noted. *Hasn't been gone that long . . . a few hours maybe. That means he died today, January 1, 2004, the first day of the New Year.*

I stayed with him for just a few more minutes, again allowing my pragmatic side to make decisions for me.

I need to cover him up, was my first thought. *I'll have to go home and get a tarp.*

I climbed back in the truck and headed for home. On a few occasions since I retired Buck, I'd thought about what I would do when this day came. I guess I'd hoped he would be at home when he passed away, not at the barn. But it didn't really matter, he was going to be buried at home regardless; that was a given.

First, I needed to find a way to get him home. My friend, Allen Jackson (not the singer), had a flatbed trailer large enough for Buck to fit on, and I was sure he'd let me borrow it.

I'll give him a call when I get home, I thought.

We were going to have to dig a grave for him, so we'd need a heavy enough backhoe to cut through the frozen and rocky ground that surrounded our house.

The rental places are closed . . . it's New Years Day. I shook my head. *I wonder if Bill is home.*

Bill Fairbanks, a friend with an excavating business and a lot of heavy machinery, was my first choice because of the love and respect he and his wife have for animals. His wife, Carolyn, runs the local animal shelter, and she and I had often debated which animal was smarter, the horse or the pig. (Of course, I said it was the horse, but she insists it's the pig!)

At any rate, by the time I got home, I had formulated a pretty solid plan for taking care of Buck's body. I parked the truck and went in the house through the back door. Wendy was in the living room. I stood for a minute, trying to think of a way to break the news.

"Buck died this morning," I said simply, as she walked toward me.

"What!" There was disbelief in her voice.

"Looks like he just lay down and went to sleep."

It was the first time I spoke the words out loud. Immediately, something in me changed. My practical side vanished, and all that was left was a fellow who had just lost the best friend, teacher, and partner he'd ever had.

"Oh . . . no." Sadness replaced the disbelief, as she quickly made her way over to me and gave me a hug.

Now, I have never really been a very outwardly emotional person, whether that emotion is anger, happiness, sadness, or whatever. Sure, I have my moments just like everybody else, but for the most part, I generally stay on a pretty even keel. But on that day, and over the days, weeks, and even months that followed, that would change. I made the phone calls to Allen and Bill, and by midafternoon Buck had taken his final trailer ride with me and was resting beneath the trees near a trail at our house, where Aaron and Buck used to ride. I have to admit, all day long it was a struggle to maintain my composure, and more times than not, it was a battle I wasn't able to win.

I truly had no idea Buck's passing would have such a profound effect on me. After all, having been around horses all my life, I was no stranger to the untimely loss of a good horse. (Thank God, it isn't a frequent occurrence, but it does happen from time to time.) When I did have to put a horse down, I was somehow able to do what needed to be done and move on without too much trouble. Don't get me wrong, losing a good horse is always a very sad proposition, and I mourned the loss every time, but this was different . . . very different.

In the weeks and months that followed, it was very difficult for me to talk about or even think about Buck without getting a little choked up. Even to this day, it isn't easy for me to discuss his passing. However, one bright spot in the whole ordeal came after Wendy wrote to three or four close friends shortly after Buck left us, to let them know he had passed away. Those friends began spreading the word in the horse community, and within a matter of days, we were receiving cards and letters of condolence from folks all over the world.

Only six months before Buck passed away, my fourth book, *Life Lessons from a Ranch Horse,* had been released. It was written as a tribute to Buck, and in it I described many of the lessons I had learned from him during the time he and I had together. Many of the people who sent cards and letters mentioned how the lessons I wrote about in the book had been of value to them, and they wanted not only to express their sadness at his passing, but they also wanted to send a thank-you to both Buck and me for sharing our experiences with them. It was truly heartwarming to find that Buck had had such a positive impact on so many people all over the world . . . people who had never even met him.

We continued to receive letters and cards about Buck clear into the summer months, and all of us here at home were very touched by the generous outpouring of sentiment for him. It didn't make me miss him any less, though.

For months, Wendy had been urging me to write something about Buck's passing to update our website, but I just couldn't bring myself to do it. As a result, the section about him on the website remained the same for nearly a year after his death. When I finally was able to write something about him, it was only a few sentences, and I haven't been able to look at his page on the website since.

In the spring or early summer of that year, we received an email from a good friend, Anita Parra, from California. She wanted to let us know her horse, Wicket, had to be put to sleep, due to some major internal problems he had been suffering from. I had met Anita and Wicket several years before, when they attended one of our clinics, and I'd always really liked him. Since that first meeting, I had the opportunity to work with the two of them on a number of occasions, including one in which we worked on helping Wicket learn to pull a cart. Over time, Anita and her husband, Carl Hill, began hosting clinics at their own place, and we all ended up being very good friends.

It was tough for me when I read Anita's email about Wicket, because I had always seen their relationship as being much like the relationship between Buck and me. Over the next several weeks, I tried a number of times to sit down and write a note of condolence to Anita, but just like trying to write the update for the website, I just couldn't bring myself to do it.

Later, in the fall of the year, my assistant, Kathleen, and I went to Anita and Carl's place to do a couple of clinics. As soon as we got there, I made a point to let Anita know how sorry I was to hear about Wicket's passing. Even that was excruciatingly difficult for me.

Over the next few days, we all settled into the routine we've developed at Anita and Carl's place whenever we do clinics there. Breakfast at about 7:00 A.M., clinic from 8:00 until whenever we're finished, and then back up to the house for chips and red-pepper dip before supper. During those times at the house around mealtime, Carl and I found ourselves becoming very good friends.

Life is fun for Carl, as it should be for all of us, and if someone isn't having fun, he feels it's his responsibility to make sure they have some. He has a very quick wit and an interesting way of looking at the world (and life in general, for that matter), which often makes for very interesting dinner conversations.

One night during our visit, we had finished supper and were sitting at the table, talking over the day's events and mixing in some funny stories about this and that, when Anita excused herself to go out and check on the clinic participants' horses. Kathleen, Carl, and I remained at the table finishing up the stories we had started. Shortly after Anita left the room, Carl suddenly became serious and began talking about the day they put Wicket to sleep.

He spoke of the circumstances leading up to it and how, just before they gave Wicket the shot that would end his life, all the other animals on the place seemed to know what was coming and, in their own way, came to say good-bye to him. We talked about how tough his passing had been on both Carl and Anita and how hard Buck's passing had been on me. Then, when it seemed we had said everything there was to say on the subject, Carl leaned forward in his chair.

"You know," he said, "it comes with the price of the ticket. When we sign on to take certain things into our lives, whether it's the job we do or the people and animals we care about, we have to understand it's not going to be good all the time. How boring a life would that be, anyway? Yeah, there's going to be a lot of good . . . like your time with Buck and the time we had with Wicket . . ."

I nodded my agreement.

"But when we buy the ticket," he continued, "we sign on for the whole package . . . the good and the not so good. It's all part of the deal. It's all in the price of the ticket. It's just the sign that we've bought into the life we've been given, and we're taking ownership of it."

He paused, as he took a sip from his glass.

"It's really not such a bad deal . . . is it?"

His analogy made me smile.

It's a funny thing, this life of ours. It's just plumb full of paths we can choose to take or choose not to take. And along with each one of those paths we choose to follow comes a variety of trade-offs. Sometimes we're going to be faced with what seems like overwhelming trials and tribulations; sometimes we will be faced with overwhelming joy and happiness. But we can always take comfort in knowing that neither one will last forever.

We can also take comfort in knowing that whether things come to us that are beneficial to our lives or things come that aren't, the only thing that really matters is what we ultimately make of it. We can look at our life's setbacks as roadblocks we can't get around or simply stumbling blocks we need to find a way to get over. Either way, the choice is up to us.

In the end, it's all just a sign that we're taking ownership of the life we've been given. And lucky for us, it all comes with the price of the ticket.

About the Author

Mark Rashid is an internationally acclaimed horse trainer known for his ability to understand the horse's point of view and solve difficult problems with communication rather than force. He began working with horses at age ten, when he met the wise "old man," who taught him to work *with* horses, not against them, and to listen to what the horse is trying to say. Mark's clinics center on one-on-one work with horse *and* rider and are immensely popular with people around the world.

When Mark decided to study the martial art of aikido as a way to improve his horsemanship, he brought the same quiet determination to it that he exhibits in his work with horses. After years of practice, he earned a black belt in Yoshinkan aikido and now trains and teaches the "way of harmony" in the local dojo.

Mark worked full time on ranches for many years gathering herds, managing stock, and training horses. When time permits, he still enjoys working on ranches near his home in Estes Park, Colorado.

Mark has been a guest on NPR's *The Horse Show,* and was featured on the *Nature* series on PBS. He is the author of four previous books, *Considering the Horse, A Good Horse Is Never a Bad Color, Horses Never Lie,* and *Life Lessons from a Ranch Horse.*